Cultivating a Flourishing Society

How We Can Build Cultures Where People Thrive

JUDD ALLEN, Ph.D.

For permission requests, bulk orders, or special sales inquiries, contact:

Human Resources Institute, LLC
HealthyCulture.com
151 Dunder Road
Burlington, Vermont 05401 USA
JuddA@healthyculture.com
(802) 862-8855

Special discounts are available for quantity purchases by organizations, associations, educational institutions, and other groups.

Library of Congress Control Number: 2026911620

ISBN 978-0-941703-58-1 (eBook)
ISBN 978-0-941703-17-8 (paperback)
ISBN 978-0-941703-57-4 (hardcover)

Cover photograph of Judd Allen by Karen Pike, of www.kpikephoto.com.

Table of Contents

Author's Preface.......v
Acknowledgements.......ix
Chapter 1: Beyond Good Intentions: Cultivating a Society Where People Thrive.......1
Part I: The Cultural Architecture of Flourishing.......11
Chapter 2: Shared Values in a Flourishing Society.......15
Chapter 3: The Role of Cultural Norms in a Flourishing Society.......29
Chapter 4: The Role of Cultural Touchpoints in a Flourishing Society.....41
Chapter 5: The Role of Peer Support in a Flourishing Society.......57
Chapter 6: The Role of Leadership Support in a Flourishing Society. 69
Chapter 7: The Role of Social Climate in a Flourishing Society.......83
Part II: Institutions and Systems – Where Culture Becomes Concrete.......97
Chapter 8: The Role of Technology and Innovation in a Flourishing Society.......103
Chapter 9: The Role of Business and Finance in a Flourishing Society.......119
Chapter 10: The Role of Families in a Flourishing Society.......133
Chapter 11: The Role of Educational Institutions in a Flourishing Society.......141
Chapter 12: The Role of Workplaces in a Flourishing Society.......153
Chapter 13: The Role of Civic and Community Organizations in a Flourishing Society.......165
Chapter 14: The Role of Healthcare in a Flourishing Society.......175
Chapter 15: The Role of Government in a Flourishing Society.......187
Part III: Cultivating A Flourishing Society Together.......199
Chapter 16: Examples of Flourishing Cultures in Action.......207

Chapter 17: Deciding Where to Begin 219
Chapter 18: Analyzing Flourishing in the Current Culture............. 231
Chapter 19: Embracing Systemic and Systematic Change 255
Chapter 20: Why Flourishing Cultures Matter: A Summary of Social Benefits and the Case for Urgency.................................... 271
Chapter 21: Cultivating a Flourishing Society: A Shared Invitation. 287

References 293

Key Intellectual Influences.. 299

Appendix: The Case for Flourishing Values 301

Author's Preface

"If we have moved ahead out of darkness, it is because a few have dared to walk together in the sun."

— George Sand (paraphrased by Robert F. Allen)

This book was written at a time when many social, economic, and technological trends feel overwhelming, and when accounts of fragmentation, alienation, insecurity, and decline dominate public conversation. It may therefore seem unusual—perhaps even unrealistic—to write about the possibility of a flourishing society.

I do so deliberately.

I came to this project not as an optimist, but as someone who grew increasingly troubled by what felt like a collective failure of imagination. Consider the parent working two jobs who still cannot afford stable housing, the teenager who has grown up more fluent in the language of anxiety than of hope, the older man in a care facility whose deepest need is to feel known by someone. These are not edge cases. They are the ordinary texture of life for millions of people—and they are, in large part, the product of choices we have made together about how to organize our common life.

For years, I have been studying how communities, institutions, and cultural norms shape whether people flourish or struggle. What struck me was not simply how much distress there was, but how routinely we treated it as a private problem rather than a public one—as though suffering were a personal failure rather than a signal that something had gone wrong in the structures around us. The question that would not leave me was this: what would a society actually look like if it were organized around human flourishing? This book is my attempt to answer it.

Periods of widespread distress invite sharp diagnosis, and much of it is warranted. Scholars, journalists, and public intellectuals have done essential work documenting the erosion of trust, community, meaning, and stability in contemporary life. But diagnosis alone is not enough. Without a clear vision of what a healthier society would look like, we are left with adaptation rather than transformation—learning to endure conditions that quietly erode mental health, dignity, connection, and a basic sense of safety. A society that cannot imagine a flourishing alternative risks normalizing its own pathology.

This book approaches utopia not as a finished blueprint or an unattainable ideal, but as a guide through turbulent times. Asking what a flourishing society would require helps us clarify human needs—not only meaning, belonging, and autonomy, but also the safety and security that make flourishing widely attainable rather than the privilege of the fortunate few. It helps us examine how culture and institutions shape daily life and identify where distress is produced by design rather than by chance. The chapters that follow move from the foundations of individual well-being—attachment, meaning, autonomy, and security—outward to the economic arrangements, civic institutions, and cultural norms that either support or undermine them. Each chapter draws on social science, philosophy, and, drawing on my own experience across four decades of applied work, the practical realities of how cultures and institutions actually change.

This book does not assume that flourishing must wait for ideal conditions. Human beings have always shown a remarkable capacity to pursue dignity, connection, and purpose even in times of instability and deprivation. The movements for abolition, for democratic self-governance, for the rights of workers and women—none waited for favorable conditions; all of them remade the conditions themselves. Yet a decent society should not depend on extraordinary resilience as the price of a meaningful life. One of the central claims of this book is that while flourishing can occur under adverse conditions, a flourishing society makes it far more possible, more sustainable, and more equitably shared.

The capacity to imagine, learn, and adapt together is itself a marker of health—for both individuals and societies. In times of rapid change, flourishing depends not on rigid stability but on the ability to reflect collectively, revise our norms, and harness new knowledge in the service of human well-being.

Writing about a flourishing society is not an act of optimism. It is a refusal to accept that the distance between the society we have inherited and the one we can make is fixed. That distance is large. But it is a measure not of impossibility—it is a measure of how much remains to be built and of what it would mean to move forward.

Acknowledgements

My family, teachers, friends, and colleagues have been steadfast champions of kindness, joy, meaningful work, learning, connection, and health. Their lives and commitments inspire me every day, and it is because of them that this book exists.

In preparing this book, I made selective use of large language model (LLM) tools to assist with brainstorming, editing, and refining the language. These tools supported the writing process but did not originate the core concepts, frameworks, or conclusions presented here, which are the result of my own work and experience.

Chapter 1

Beyond Good Intentions: Cultivating a Society Where People Thrive

The test of a good society is not whether it avoids difficulty but whether it creates the conditions for people to meet difficulty well.

— Paraphrase of Erich Fromm, The Sane Society

Designing a Flourishing Society

We live in a time of extraordinary achievement and persistent strain. Our technologies are more advanced than ever. Our knowledge has expanded dramatically. Our institutions are complex and powerful. Yet many people report rising anxiety, isolation, burnout, and fragmentation.

It is tempting to interpret these patterns as personal shortcomings or as inevitable features of modern life. But there is another possibility—and it is the premise of this book: many of the pressures we face are not merely individual problems but signals of cultural misalignment. The systems we have built—our institutions, norms, financial structures, technologies, and leadership patterns—may not yet align with fundamental human needs.

This misalignment is not a new observation. What is new is the convergence of tools—from organizational psychology to behavioral economics to network science—that allow us to do something about it. Dozens of books have diagnosed modern society's discontents. This book asks a different question and attempts a bolder task:

> *What would it look like to deliberately build a flourishing society—and how would we actually go about doing it?*

That shift from diagnosis to design is what sets this work apart. Drawing on Kurt Lewin's action research tradition, Robert F. Allen's normative systems framework, and a growing body of evidence from the social sciences, this book offers a practical architecture for cultural change—not just a description of what is wrong but a working method for making it better.

From Survival to Flourishing: A Three-Level Framework

To understand what flourishing means, it helps to contrast it with two more familiar ways of organizing social life.

A survival mindset organizes culture around threat reduction: minimizing risk, coping with stress, and avoiding harm. It is reactive by nature. A sanity framework raises the bar—reducing dysfunction, correcting distortions, restoring a baseline of normalcy. Both are necessary—but neither is sufficient.

Flourishing goes further. It asks not just "what prevents people from falling apart?" but "what conditions help people grow, contribute, connect, and find meaning?" It integrates well-being, purpose, learning, joy, dignity, and mutual support into a coherent aspiration—for individuals and for society as a whole.

This distinction matters because it changes what we design for. A survival culture builds walls. A sane culture repairs damage. A flourishing culture cultivates the soil. When we orient institutions, norms, and leadership practices toward flourishing, we are not simply preventing people from falling apart—we are actively helping them develop strengths, deepen relationships, and build shared capacity. The bar is higher, and so is the reward.

The Social Foundations of Flourishing

The ideas in this book draw on a long intellectual tradition that recognizes culture as a decisive factor in personal and civic well-being. In *The Sane Society*, Erich Fromm argued that distress often reflects maladaptive cultural arrangements rather than individual defects. When societies prioritize competition over connection, consumption over meaning, and status over dignity, alienation becomes predictable. In this view, mental health is not solely a clinical matter; it is a social achievement.

In *The Civic Culture*, political scientists Gabriel Almond and Sidney Verba extended this insight, showing that democratic stability depends on supportive civic norms—trust, moderation, participation, and belief in political efficacy. Institutions alone do not sustain democracy; they require a culture that legitimizes participation while containing polarization. Later, in *Bowling Alone*, Robert Putnam documented the erosion of social capital: declining participation in associations, weakening community bonds, and shrinking networks of trust. As those connective tissues fray, civic life and individual well-being decline together. In *The*

Good Society, Robert Bellah and colleagues warned that excessive individualism and market logic were crowding out the moral commitments necessary for common life.

Yet diagnosing cultural decline is only part of the task. The crucial question is whether culture can be intentionally reshaped. Here, Kurt Lewin's work is foundational. Lewin's field theory holds that behavior is a function of both the person and their environment. To achieve different outcomes, we must change the field in which people live and act. Lewin pioneered action research—a disciplined, iterative process that diagnoses social conditions, tests interventions, measures results, and refines practice. It is a scientific method applied not to the laboratory but to culture itself.

Building on Lewin's insight, Robert F. Allen offered a practical architecture for cultural change through his work on Normative Systems and in *The Organizational Unconscious*. Allen argued that every group operates within a largely invisible normative system—a patterned set of shared expectations, reinforcements, informal rules, and emotional undercurrents that quietly govern behavior. These norms are sustained not only by formal policies but by daily signals about what is noticed, rewarded, ignored, or sanctioned.

Attempts at reform that focus solely on individual motivation or surface-level policy shifts often fail when the underlying normative system remains intact. Culture change requires making implicit rules visible, identifying leverage points within the system, and realigning reinforcement patterns so that desired values and behaviors become normative rather than exceptional.

This book builds on that lineage. If psychological health, democratic vitality, and social trust depend on cultural conditions, then flourishing must be cultivated systematically—not wished for and not left to chance.

We Can Create Supportive Cultural Environments

Cultures are complex webs of social influences that shape attitudes and behaviors. Subcultures are localized expressions of that web—in households, families, friendship networks, workplaces, neighborhoods, towns, cities, states, and regions. They are where culture becomes daily life: what is modeled, expected, reinforced, and taken for granted.

Each subculture can be understood through six interacting elements that together form its architecture:

- **Shared values** – the priorities consistently elevated and protected
- **Norms** – the everyday expectations that guide behavior
- **Peer support** – how people encourage, guide, and hold one another accountable
- **Leadership support** – how formal and informal leaders model values, align systems, and remove barriers
- **Touchpoints** – the recurring policies, practices, incentives, symbols, and environments that reinforce culture
- **Social climate** – the lived experience of trust, belonging, safety, and realistic hope

These elements do not operate independently. They form a system. When aligned, they reduce the psychological effort required to live well. When misaligned, individuals are left to privately compensate for systemic contradictions—an exhausting and ultimately futile task.

Think of these strands as a spider's web. When they align around limiting patterns, they exert a steady pull on group members. Even highly motivated individuals often find themselves drawn back into familiar attitudes and behaviors, because the surrounding web quietly rewards conformity and subtly penalizes deviation. This is why willpower alone is rarely strong enough to counteract a coordinated system of expectations and reinforcements. Sustainable transformation requires adjusting multiple strands at once so that new behaviors are supported rather than resisted by the surrounding culture.

This is also why subcultures matter so much. Within circles of friends, households, workgroups, families, and neighborhoods, people can intentionally cultivate healthier expectations and trusting climates. These microcultures become protective spaces where dignity is reinforced, and encouragement is consistent. Over time, they can influence adjacent networks, gradually reshaping the larger web from the inside out. You do not need to change the whole of society to begin. You need to change the field around you.

Institutions as Stewards of Flourishing

Social institutions carry these cultural elements at scale. They shape development across the lifespan, distribute opportunities, define accountability, and stabilize collective life. For better and for worse, institutions can foster flourishing—or normalize chronic strain.

When aligned with shared values and a healthy social climate, institutions reduce isolation and insecurity, support learning and development, protect dignity during times of vulnerability, distribute opportunities more equitably, and strengthen collective resilience. When misaligned, they may inadvertently amplify stress, inequity, or cynicism—even when they appear functional from the outside.

A flourishing society expects its institutions to be reflective, humane, future-oriented, and capable of systemic cultural change.

Institutions are not static structures. They are stewards of collective well-being across generations, and they can be redesigned.

Why This Book, and Why Now

There is no shortage of books about what is wrong with modern society. What is rarer—and what this book attempts—is a practical framework for what to do about it.

The convergence of several developments makes this moment particularly consequential. Social trust has eroded measurably across many democracies. Technology is reshaping the norms of attention, connection, and work faster than institutions can adapt. The COVID-19 pandemic forced a global confrontation with questions about collective well-being that remain inadequately answered. And a generation of young people is navigating these conditions without robust cultural scaffolding.

At the same time, we know more than ever before about how culture actually works—how norms form and shift, how social networks transmit behavior, how institutions can be redesigned to align with human flourishing rather than against it. The tools exist. What has been missing is an integrated framework for applying them.

That is what this book provides: not a utopian vision but a working method—grounded in social science, tested in practice, and oriented toward the concrete question of how communities, institutions, and societies can be deliberately shaped to support human flourishing.

An Invitation to Participate

The vision described here may sound ambitious. In one sense, it is. But it is a grounded ambition, built from observable cultural elements and practical processes of change—not from wishful thinking.

This work begins wherever people gather: in families, workplaces, classrooms, community organizations, financial institutions, technology firms, and government. No one builds a flourishing society alone. It requires people willing to examine culture honestly, align systems with shared values, strengthen peer relationships, steward innovation responsibly, and think beyond immediate pressures.

The invitation is not abstract. It is specific: examine the subculture you are part of right now. What does it actually reward? What does it subtly penalize? What would need to shift for it to become a place where people genuinely flourish? Those questions—and the discipline to answer them honestly and act on what you find—are where this work begins.

Do not accept cultural strain as the inevitable price of modern life. Begin where you have influence. Align the touchpoints you can touch. Strengthen the relationships you are part of. Encourage institutions to act as stewards of flourishing. Join with others in shaping conditions that support health, learning, connection, and meaningful contribution.

Flourishing is not accidental. It is designed, reinforced, and continually renewed. And it is possible.

How This Book is Organized

To explore how a flourishing society can be cultivated, this book is organized into three interconnected parts.

Part I: The Cultural Architecture of Flourishing

This section examines the six foundational cultural elements that shape daily life: shared values, norms, peer support, leadership support, touchpoints, and social climate. These elements form an interconnected system. When aligned, they reduce the psychological effort required to live well. When misaligned, individuals must privately compensate for systemic contradictions. Part I provides the conceptual foundation for everything that follows.

Part II: Institutions and Systems – Where Culture Becomes Concrete

This section examines the major social institutions that carry culture at scale—families, schools, workplaces, healthcare systems, governments, civic organizations, financial systems, and technology sectors. These institutions distribute opportunity, shape development across the lifespan, and define accountability. When aligned with flourishing values, they strengthen dignity, learning, connection, and resilience. When misaligned, they normalize chronic strain. Part II shows how each institution can be reimagined as a steward of flourishing rather than a source of it.

Part III: Cultivating a Flourishing Society Together

The final section addresses the practical question of how we move forward together. Cultural transformation is not imposed from above; it is cultivated through participation. This section explores pathways for collaborative action—within subcultures, across institutions, and through civic engagement. Drawing on action research and normative systems theory, it outlines how intentional, evidence-informed cultural change can move subcultures—and eventually broader society—toward greater alignment with human flourishing.

Flourishing societies are not discovered. They are built through honest examination, deliberate design, and sustained collective effort. That work is what this book is about. Let us begin.

PART I
THE CULTURAL ARCHITECTURE OF FLOURISHING

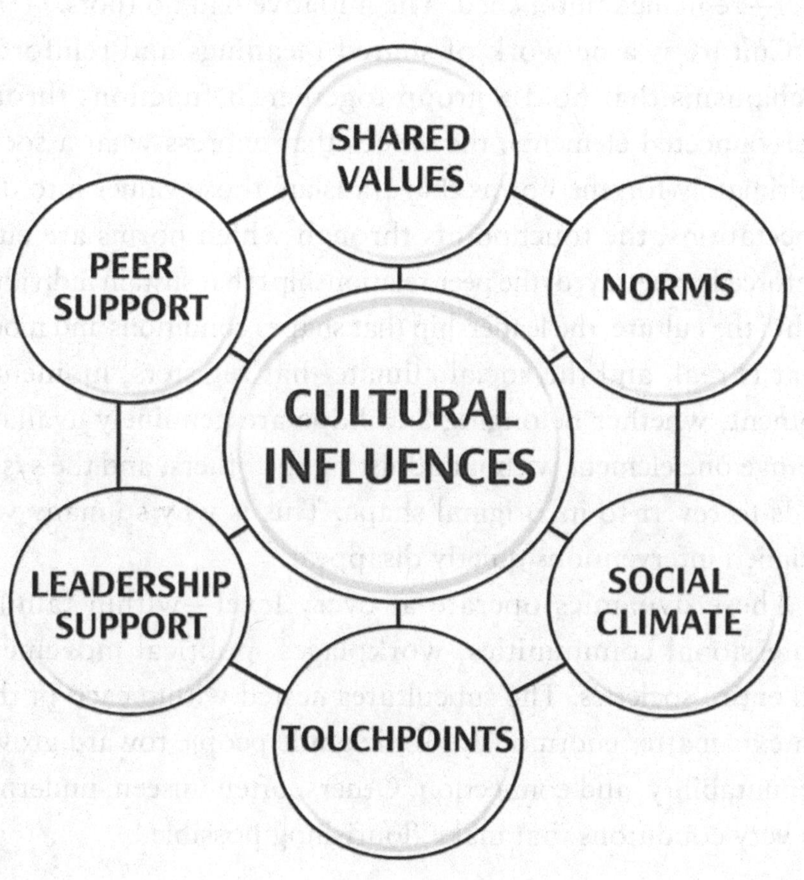

Many efforts for social reform target individuals—promoting better choices, increased resilience, or stronger coping skills. Others focus solely on policies. Both approaches, however well-intentioned, often neglect the larger system quietly shaping behavior from beneath: culture.

Consider a workplace where a new well-being initiative launches with fanfare—workshops, posters, and a dedicated Slack channel. Within months, it fades. Not because people didn't care but because the surrounding culture—the unspoken expectations, the way leaders actually behaved, the stories colleagues told each other—remained untouched. The initiative had no roots.

Culture is a network of shared meanings and reinforcing mechanisms that hold a group together. It functions through interconnected elements: the values that express what a society is ultimately for, the norms that translate those values into daily expectations, the touchpoints through which norms are either reinforced or betrayed, the peer relationships that sustain individuals within the culture, the leadership that shapes conditions and models what is real, and the social climate that registers, moment to moment, whether belonging and hope are genuinely available. Change one element without adjusting the others, and the system tends to revert to its original shape. This is why so many well-designed interventions quietly disappear.

These dynamics operate at every level—within families, professional communities, workplaces, political movements, and entire societies. The subcultures nested within each of these contexts matter enormously. Some guide people toward growth, accountability, and connection. Others, often unseen, undermine the very conditions that make flourishing possible.

In the chapters ahead, I examine these six elements of culture as an interconnected system rather than isolated levers. Understanding them is the first step toward something ambitious: shaping culture with intention, at scale, in service of human flourishing. But culture is held in place—and carried forward—by the institutions and systems through which social life is organized. That is the focus of Section II. In Section III, attention turns to cultural change—the practical and demanding work of translating this vision into a systematic approach that is both systemic and grounded in the everyday reality of people's lives, relationships, and institutions.

Chapter 2

Shared Values in a Flourishing Society

WE USUALLY SEE values as personal qualities—principles that influence individual decisions and actions. However, societies, organizations, and communities also operate on shared values, often expressed more practically as priorities. These shared values are revealed not only through words but also in what gets funded, rewarded, protected, and tolerated.

In a flourishing society, certain values consistently guide collective decision-making. While these values don't need to be emphasized equally in every situation, they serve as steady reference points. When trade-offs arise, these values help determine what to keep, what to change, and which costs are unacceptable. In this way, shared values act as a moral and psychological guide—quietly shaping culture and institutions and showing what a society ultimately stands for.

This chapter examines six core values essential for flourishing: productive work, health, joy, kindness, learning, and connection. These are not just abstract ideals or personal preferences; they are collective commitments that shape culture and influence whether well-being is maintained or quietly diminished. A common question is: why these six? The answer is not that other values—such as justice, freedom, or beauty—are unimportant. Instead, these six form a practical cluster: they are mutually reinforcing, operate at both the individual and institutional levels, and their presence or absence can be observed in how people actually live. Together, they describe the conditions under which people can find purpose—a shared sense of direction and meaningful involvement in something greater than themselves.

1. Productive Work: Contribution with Dignity

In a flourishing society, work is seen as a form of community participation—not merely a means of survival or a source of status. People want their work to be useful, meaningful, and recognized as a genuine contribution to something larger than a paycheck.

Consider how this plays out in a hospital. Patient outcomes depend not only on the skill of surgeons but on the attentiveness of nurses, the cleanliness maintained by housekeeping staff, the accuracy of administrators scheduling follow-up care, and the warmth of the person who brings a meal tray. A flourishing institution understands this interdependence: every role is treated as integral rather than incidental. Employees are given meaningful autonomy, opportunities to develop their skills, and a clear sense of how their daily work makes a difference. Performance is measured not only by speed or volume but by quality, sustainability, and human impact.

Conventional economic frameworks tend to equate productivity with paid labor and market output. Work that earns wages is counted; work that sustains families and communities often is not. But a flourishing society recognizes a broader definition: productive work is any sustained effort that creates long-term value for individuals, families, communities, or future generations. Raising children, caring for aging parents, maintaining a neighborhood—these are forms of work that a healthy society notices and supports.

When work consistently requires emotional suppression, endless repetition without purpose, or permanent insecurity, psychological harm follows. A flourishing society does not treat this as a personal failing. It reads widespread demoralization at work as a signal that work conditions need to be redesigned.

> ***Diagnostic signal:*** *When work consistently feels meaningless or dehumanizing, the cultural conditions are not aligned with flourishing.*

2. Health: A Shared Responsibility

In a flourishing society, health is not treated as a personal accomplishment or a measure of moral character. Instead, it is understood as something that emerges from supportive conditions—economic, social, environmental, and relational. A person's health reflects the air they breathe, the safety of their neighborhood, the quality of their relationships, and whether they have had access to care when needed. Treating illness as purely individual ignores this reality.

Healthcare systems focused on flourishing prioritize prevention, early intervention, and continuous care. Mental health services are integrated into primary care, schools, and workplaces—rather than being isolated in stigmatized specialty settings. Seeking help early is encouraged and rewarded, not penalized or met with shame.

Public policy reflects this value through investments in clean air and water, safe housing, walkable neighborhoods, and access to nutritious food. Workplaces demonstrate it by protecting time for rest and recovery—recognizing that chronic exhaustion is a system failure, not a badge of dedication.

Perhaps most importantly, health becomes a common topic in daily life. Conversations about stress, fatigue, and mental well-being are routine rather than exceptional. In such a society, people are not left to manage quietly while pretending all is well.

> ***Diagnostic signal:*** *When burnout and illness are widespread yet treated as individual problems, the culture's design demands attention.*

3. Joy: The Capacity for Aliveness

Joy is sometimes dismissed as a luxury—pleasant when available but secondary to serious concerns like productivity or security. This is a mistake. A society's relationship with joy reveals a lot about its emotional vitality and long-term resilience. Where joy is missing or considered frivolous, something vital has been lost.

Consider what institutionalized joy actually looks like. The Danish concept of hygge—a word roughly translated as coziness or communal warmth—describes a cultural practice of intentionally creating space for shared pleasure: candles, shared meals, unhurried conversation. It is not just a personal habit but a social norm, one that shapes how Danes design homes, structure workplaces, and think about the rhythm of the year. Likewise, cities that invest in public plazas, outdoor markets, festivals, and free cultural events are making a structural choice: they are designing for gathering, not just transit.

In schools, joy is present when time is deliberately set aside for play, creative exploration, and curiosity-driven inquiry. Research consistently shows that joy enhances learning—it is not a distraction from education but a condition for it. In workplaces, joy appears in shared humor, recognition of achievements, and the simple pleasure of enjoying one's colleagues. None of this requires abandoning seriousness. Joy doesn't mean constant happiness; it means that alongside responsibility and difficulty, there is genuine space for delight.

A society that sacrifices joy entirely in pursuit of efficiency gradually depletes its emotional reserves—and discovers, too late, that resilience requires more than discipline.

> ***Diagnostic signal:*** *A society that cannot sustain joy may be emotionally depleted and more brittle in the face of hardship.*

4. Kindness: Embedded in Systems

In a flourishing society, kindness is not just a trait of caring individuals—it is structurally reinforced through the systems people encounter every day. The question is not only whether people are kind to one another in personal interactions but whether the institutions that govern their lives are designed with kindness in mind.

Social services centered on kindness are accessible without being demeaning. Administrative procedures are clear and respectful, not intentionally confusing. Legal systems focus on proportionality and fairness. Schools adopt restorative approaches to conflict rather than humiliation or harsh punishment. Workplaces view mistakes as learning opportunities—chances to understand what went wrong and improve, rather than moments for blame.

When kindness is built into institutional design, trust grows throughout society. People are more willing to ask for help, take risks, cooperate with strangers, and accept responsibility for their actions. This is not softness—it's a stabilizing force. Fear leads to defensiveness and hiding the truth. Kindness encourages openness and accountability. In this way, institutionalized kindness is one of the most practical investments a society can make.

> ***Diagnostic signal:*** *Routine experiences of humiliation, indifference, or bureaucratic coldness in public institutions indicate a misalignment with this value.*

5. Learning: The Capacity to Evolve

A flourishing society treats learning not as a phase of life that ends with formal schooling but as a continuous, collective capacity—the ability to absorb new information, revise beliefs in light of evidence, and adapt thoughtfully to new circumstances.

Educational institutions that embody this value prioritize curiosity, critical thinking, and ethical reflection over rote compliance. Students are encouraged to debate, question assumptions, and apply knowledge to real and shifting challenges—not merely to reproduce correct answers on standardized tests. This foundation matters because it shapes what kind of citizens and colleagues people become.

In workplaces, learning appears through mentorship, ongoing training, and genuine openness to innovation. Employees are proactively supported in updating their skills as technologies and conditions evolve. Importantly, organizations evaluate not only outcomes but also the quality of their reasoning during the process: what did we learn from this experience, and what would we do differently?

At the societal level, the capacity to learn is visible in how public challenges are addressed. Policies are revised when new evidence warrants it. Mistakes—even significant ones—are acknowledged rather than defended. Disagreement is seen as a source of useful information rather than a threat to suppress. In a flourishing society, dialogue is prized more than the appearance of certainty. The willingness to be wrong, to revise, and to try again is not weakness—it is the foundation of long-term collective intelligence.

> ***Diagnostic signal:*** *An inability to revise assumptions or acknowledge errors—whether in individuals, institutions, or public discourse—signals cultural rigidity that impedes adaptation.*

6. Connection: The Social Infrastructure of Well-Being

Connection is the value that plays an important role in all the others. Consider what each of the preceding values looks like when connection is stripped away. Without connection, productive work loses its sense of contribution: you may complete tasks, but there is no one to matter to or a community to serve. Health becomes fragile: research on loneliness shows it is as damaging to physical health as smoking fifteen cigarettes a day, and far more common. Joy collapses without others to share it with—delight in isolation becomes sadness. Kindness has no recipient, and therefore no function. Learning turns defensive: people who feel socially unsafe stop admitting what they do not know. In each case, the value depends on relationship to survive.

A flourishing society recognizes this and invests accordingly. Neighborhoods are designed to encourage spontaneous interactions instead of private enclaves. Workplaces foster genuine collaboration rather than the competitive individualism that makes people feel expendable. Families and caregivers are supported rather than left to shoulder their burdens alone.

Institutions build trust by being transparent and responsive—acting as if the people they serve truly matter. Public discourse highlights a shared understanding of facts and values rather than viewing every difference as a battle to win. In a connected society, conflict isn't eliminated; it is made manageable. People who feel they belong are much more likely to stay engaged when disagreements arise, listen across differences, and work through difficulties rather than withdraw or retaliate.

> ***Diagnostic signal:*** *Chronic loneliness and deep social polarization are not personal failures—they are structural signals that connection has been inadequately supported.*

Living the Values Together

These six values do not operate independently. Together, they form a system that reinforces and deepens the others. They are not merely ideals to aspire toward but the living core of a flourishing culture (Readers seeking a fuller treatment of each value and its distinctive contribution will find it in the Appendix).

Productive work preserves dignity, which makes people healthier. Good health enables participation, which deepens connection. Connection creates the conditions for joy—and for the safety that learning requires. Kindness is both expressed through and sustained by all of the above. Each value, when present, makes the others more achievable; each, when absent, weakens the rest.

When these values are fully embedded in culture and institutions—not just cited in mission statements but visible in how resources are allocated, how conflicts are resolved, how mistakes are treated—people experience society as something they belong to. Something they can shape and improve. Something worth contributing to.

When they are absent or weak, individuals are left to fill cultural gaps on their own. They carry the weight of what institutions have failed to provide—and they carry it quietly, because asking for more is often treated as a personal complaint rather than legitimate social feedback.

A flourishing society does not eliminate hardship or uncertainty. Instead, it fosters the cultural and institutional conditions that help people face challenges together—with resilience, creativity, and compassion. The goal is not perfection. It is the capacity to recognize when something is wrong, to honestly identify it, and work toward something better.

Diagnostic Questions: Assessing Shared Values in Practice

The following questions are meant to stimulate reflection on whether a society—or any part of it—is actively upholding the values described in this chapter. There is no scoring system. The goal is honest inquiry, not measurement. Patterns over time matter more than any single observation.

Productive Work

- Does work support meaningful contribution and dignity?
- Do most people have access to roles that feel useful and socially valued?

- Can individuals see how their work contributes beyond personal gain?
- Do workplaces support autonomy, skill development, and mastery?
- Are workers treated as contributors whose well-being matters—or as replaceable inputs?
- Is unpaid but essential work recognized and supported?

***Diagnostic signal:** When work consistently feels meaningless or dehumanizing, the conditions are not aligned with flourishing.*

Health

- Is health treated as a shared responsibility rather than a personal achievement?
- Are physical and mental health services accessible and integrated?
- Are prevention and early support prioritized?
- Do cultural norms promote rest and recovery—or glorify exhaustion?
- Are environments designed to reduce chronic stress?
- Can people seek help without fear of stigma or penalty?

***Diagnostic signal:** When burnout and illness are prevalent but viewed as personal failings, the culture requires attention.*

Joy

- Is there genuine space for vitality, play, and shared celebration?
- Do people have time for creativity and curiosity?

- Are art, humor, and beauty publicly valued—not merely tolerated?
- Are moments of shared achievement common and recognized?
- Is joy treated as legitimate, or as an indulgence to be deferred indefinitely?

Diagnostic signal: *A society that cannot sustain joy may be emotionally drained and more vulnerable than it seems.*

Kindness

- Do institutions treat people with consistent respect and fairness?
- Are mistakes met with learning rather than automatic punishment?
- Do people feel safe asking for help?
- Is trust a reasonable expectation in daily life—or a naïve one?
- Is kindness modeled at the highest levels of public and institutional life?

Diagnostic signal: *Routine experiences of humiliation or indifference indicate a serious cultural misalignment.*

Learning

- Are curiosity and critical thinking genuinely encouraged?
- Do institutions revise policies in response to new evidence?
- Is disagreement used to foster inquiry rather than suppress it?

- Are people actively supported in adapting to new technologies and changing conditions?
- Is admitting error treated as a sign of integrity—or as vulnerability to be exploited?

***Diagnostic signal:** An inability to revise assumptions or acknowledge mistakes shows cultural rigidity that will hinder growth.*

Connection

- Do people experience meaningful relationships—in neighborhoods, workplaces, and communities?
- Are public and social spaces designed to encourage interaction?
- Do institutions assist people in building a shared understanding of facts, values, and priorities?
- Are differences navigated through dialogue rather than weaponized for division?
- Do people feel they belong to something larger than themselves?

***Diagnostic signal:** Chronic loneliness and polarization are not personal failures; they are cultural issues that require cultural solutions.*

Integrative Questions

Beyond each value, a flourishing society can be assessed by asking how these values function together:

- Do these values reinforce each other, or do institutions pit them against one another?

- Do people feel that they belong to something larger than themselves?
- Is there a shared sense of purpose and direction—even amid genuine disagreement?
- Can society respond effectively to new challenges together?
- Is distress—individual or collective—treated as feedback worth learning from?

A Note on Using This Diagnostic

These questions aim to encourage reflection and honest dialogue, not to generate a numerical score. A society's true measure is not how close it is to an ideal but its ability to recognize its own flaws, learn from them, and adapt its institutions to reflect shared values. The goal is not a perfect society—it is a self-aware and responsive one.

Chapter 3

The Role of Cultural Norms in a Flourishing Society

EVERY SOCIETY DEPENDS on cultural norms—shared expectations about behavior, interaction, and responsibility—to operate smoothly. Without norms, social life becomes unpredictable and tiring. People are left unsure of what is expected, what is acceptable, and what will be met with support or punishment. In extreme cases, the absence of shared norms leads to anomie: a state of normlessness in which individuals feel unanchored, anxious, and disconnected from the community.

A flourishing society prevents anomie by providing people with a supportive normative framework—enough shared expectations to foster stability, trust, and coherence. At the same time, it avoids the opposite risk: strict or punitive norms that stifle individuality, generate ongoing anxiety, or enforce conformity at the expense of human diversity. The key question is not whether norms are necessary but which norms most effectively support dignity, mental health, and collective capacity. The history of social institutions offers instructive contrasts. Anthropologist Ruth Benedict, writing in the mid-twentieth century, observed that societies differ dramatically not just in what norms they hold but in how those norms are transmitted and enforced—whether through shame and surveillance or through internalized pride and communal belonging. More recently, organizational psychologist Amy Edmondson's research on high-performing hospital teams found that units with norms of psychological safety—where asking questions and admitting errors were encouraged rather than punished—made fewer serious medical mistakes and adapted more effectively to crises. The norms themselves, not just the individuals within a system, shaped what was possible.

Norms as Invisible Infrastructure

Cultural norms largely function beneath conscious awareness. They shape how people speak to one another, how mistakes are handled, how differences are addressed, and how power is exercised. Norms tell us:

- when to speak and when to listen,
- what kinds of effort are respected,
- how conflict is managed, and
- what emotions are acceptable to express.

In a flourishing society, norms function as **invisible infrastructure**—quietly reducing friction, easing social anxiety, and facilitating cooperation. People do not have to constantly look out for danger or approval; they can relax into participation because expectations are clear, humane, and predictable.

Avoiding Anomie Without Creating Oppression

Too few norms leave people feeling unanchored. Too many—or norms enforced without compassion—leave people constrained. A flourishing society strikes a balance by ensuring that norms:

- provide guidance rather than surveillance,
- encourage participation rather than mere compliance, and
- support growth rather than punish deviation.

Healthy norms reduce uncertainty without removing choice. They provide guidance, not scripts. People know what is generally expected, but they can still express their personality, creativity, and diverse abilities.

Importantly, norms in a flourishing society are proportionate. Minor deviations are met with tolerance or gentle correction, not shame or exclusion. Serious harm is addressed firmly but with an emphasis on accountability and repair rather than humiliation. This raises a genuinely difficult question that a flourishing society cannot avoid: who decides when a norm has shifted from guidance into control? Norms are not neutral instruments. They are shaped by those with the power to define what is "normal," and historically, dominant groups have encoded their own preferences as universal standards. A flourishing society, therefore, requires not just good norms but ongoing mechanisms for questioning them—spaces in which those most affected by a norm can name its costs and propose revisions. This is not a threat to social cohesion; it is one of the conditions that make genuine cohesion possible.

Norms That Support Self-Expression and Diversity

A flourishing society recognizes that people differ widely in temperament, ability, background, identity, and pace of development. Its norms are therefore flexible enough to accommodate this variation without sacrificing coherence. One of the clearest indicators of flourishing norms is psychological safety—the felt sense of being able to participate without undue fear of embarrassment, rejection, or punishment.

This means norms that:

- allow multiple ways of contributing,
- recognize different forms of competence,
- accommodate disability and difference without stigma, and
- avoid narrow definitions of success or worth.

For instance, norms around participation may emphasize contribution without mandating a single communication style. Productivity norms may prioritize usefulness and craftsmanship over constant visibility or speed. Norms around emotional expression may allow both enthusiasm and quiet presence.

Such norms reduce performance anxiety and help bring individuals' full selves into shared spaces.

Norms as Expressions of Flourishing Values

In a flourishing society, cultural norms express the culture's commitment to **productive work, health, joy, kindness, learning, and connection.** If values articulate what a society cares about, norms reveal how those values are lived day to day. In a flourishing society, there is alignment between the two.

For example, if a society values learning, that value becomes visible through norms such as:

- asking questions is encouraged rather than penalized,
- admitting uncertainty is seen as responsible rather than weak,
- mistakes are treated as opportunities for learning,
- feedback is offered constructively, and
- changing one's mind in light of new evidence is respected.

When values and norms diverge—when learning is praised rhetorically but punished behaviorally—people become cynical, guarded, and disengaged. Flourishing requires cultural integrity: **the daily experience must match the declared priorities.**

Examples of Value-Consistent Norms

To illustrate how shared values become lived norms in a flourishing society, consider the following:

- **Productive Work**
  Norms emphasize doing work well rather than merely appearing busy. Collaboration is valued over internal competition. Pride in craft is respected. Unpaid but essential work—caregiving, mentoring, community service—is recognized and supported.
- **Health**
  Norms make it acceptable to rest, seek help, and set limits. Overwork is not glorified. Conversations about stress and well-being are ordinary. People are not expected to perform while ill as proof of commitment.
- **Joy**
  Norms allow humor, celebration, and play in appropriate contexts. Enjoyment is not treated as unprofessional or frivolous. Shared pleasure is understood as strengthening relationships and morale.
- **Kindness**
  Norms favor respectful communication, patience, and fairness. Vulnerability is met with support rather than exploitation. Power is exercised with accountability and care.
- **Learning**
  Norms encourage curiosity, reflection, and openness. Questions are welcome. Mistakes are discussed without shame. Growth is expected throughout life.

- **Connection**
  Norms promote inclusion, cooperation, and shared responsibility. People greet each other, notice when someone is absent, and create space for participation. Differences are addressed through dialogue rather than ignored or attacked.

Living Norms, not Static Rules

Finally, norms in a flourishing society are dynamic. They are reviewed, discussed, and adjusted as conditions and understandings evolve. They are shaped through dialogue rather than imposed unilaterally. This reflective capacity is one of the key strengths of flourishing: **a society grows when it can examine its own expectations and improve them.**

A flourishing society does not cling rigidly to tradition, nor does it abandon structure in the name of freedom. It recognizes that people thrive when expectations are clear, humane, and flexible—when norms guide behavior without constraining humanity.

In this way, cultural norms become the terrain on which the promise of a flourishing society is either kept or betrayed. When norms are humane, clear, and open to revision, they resolve the central tension this chapter began with: they hold anomie at bay without tipping into oppression. When they are rigid, exclusionary, or dishonest about the power they serve, they do the opposite—producing the very anxiety and disconnection they claim to prevent. The work of building a flourishing society is, in no small part, the ongoing work of getting its norms right.

Subcultures as Engines of Expression and Renewal

A flourishing society does not require uniformity of norms across all groups and settings. Instead, it allows—and even expects—the emergence of **subcultures:** communities, professions, neighborhoods, and movements that adopt distinctive norms while remaining aligned with shared values.

These subcultures provide essential flexibility within the larger culture. They allow people with common identities, interests, histories, or occupations to shape norms that suit their specific context—how they collaborate, communicate, learn, or express creativity—without abandoning the values that hold society together. In this way, subcultures prevent shared norms from becoming rigid or overly generalized.

In a flourishing society, subcultures serve as testing grounds for the expression of values. Groups experiment with new ways of embodying productive work, learning, kindness, health, joy, or connection. Some experiments remain local; others reveal more effective, humane, or inclusive practices that can be adopted more widely. What begins as a subcultural norm may, over time, refine mainstream understanding of what shared values look like in practice.

Importantly, the relationship between subcultures and the broader society is characterized by mutual respect rather than suspicion. Distinctive norms are not automatically treated as deviant, nor are they uncritically romanticized. They are evaluated by their consistency with core values—specifically, their support for dignity, well-being, and collective capacity. This evaluation is not always easy. When a subculture's norms appear to conflict with mainstream expectations—when, for instance, a professional community develops norms of blunt dissent, or a neighborhood maintains practices that outsiders misread as disorder—the default response in a flourishing society is curiosity, not enforcement. The question asked is not "does this fit our existing template?" but "does this serve the people involved, and does it do so without undermining others?" This slower, more deliberate judgment is one of the things that distinguishes a flourishing society from one that merely tolerates difference on its surface while quietly marginalizing it.

When subcultures are suppressed, societies stagnate. When they flourish without shared values, societies fragment. A flourishing society avoids both outcomes by maintaining a clear value framework with normative flexibility—allowing diversity of expression while preserving coherence and trust.

Diagnostic Checklist: Healthy vs. Unhealthy Cultural Norms

Use the following questions to assess whether norms in a group, organization, or society are supporting dignity, well-being, and effective participation—or quietly undermining them. Look for patterns, not isolated incidents.

1. Clarity vs. Confusion

Healthy norms

- Expectations are clear and widely understood
- People know what is encouraged, discouraged, and negotiable
- New members can learn the norms without excessive trial and error

Unhealthy norms

- Expectations are vague, inconsistent, or hidden
- Rules applied unevenly or unpredictably
- People rely on guesswork to avoid trouble

Diagnostic signal: Chronic uncertainty increases anxiety and withdrawal.

2. Guidance vs. Control

Healthy norms

- Guide behavior without excessive monitoring
- People feel oriented rather than surveilled
- Deviations met with curiosity or gentle correction

Unhealthy norms

- Norms function primarily to control or discipline
- Surveillance or social policing is common
- Fear of being "out of bounds" dominates behavior

Diagnostic signal: Control-based norms suppress initiative and authenticity.

3. Flexibility vs. Rigidity

Healthy norms

- Allow multiple ways of contributing and belonging
- Adapt to context, role, and individual capacity
- Are revisited and revised when conditions change

Unhealthy norms

- Enforce one "right way" to participate or succeed
- Penalize difference or nonconformity
- Persist even when clearly harmful

Diagnostic signal: Rigid norms produce stress, exclusion, and stagnation.

4. Learning Orientation vs. Blame Orientation

Healthy norms

- Treat errors as opportunities to learn and improve
- Emphasize reflection, feedback, and growth
- Encourage people to change their minds based on evidence

Unhealthy norms

- Focus on fault-finding and punishment
- Discourage experimentation or risk-taking
- Treat uncertainty as incompetence

Diagnostic signal: Blame cultures produce defensiveness and stagnation.

5. Alignment With Flourishing Values vs. Value Drift

Healthy norms

- Clearly express stated values in daily practice
- Reinforce dignity, kindness, joy, learning, and connection
- Are consistent across words, actions, and incentives

Unhealthy norms

- Contradict stated values in daily practice
- Reward behavior that undermines trust and well-being
- Produce cynicism and disengagement

Diagnostic signal: Misalignment erodes credibility and morale. This is often as damaging as openly held bad values, because it produces cynicism rather than resistance. An organization that says it values work-life balance but rewards those who never disconnect teaches its members not to trust stated commitments. This is one reason why flourishing societies and institutions attend carefully to the gap between what they say and what they actually incentivize.

6. Inclusion vs. Exclusion

Healthy norms

- Make room for diversity of background, ability, and style
- Support participation by those with different needs
- Treat differences as a resource rather than a threat

Unhealthy norms

- Favor a narrow profile of "fit"
- Marginalize or make invisibleain groups
- Expect assimilation rather than mutual adaptation.

Diagnostic signal: Exclusion weakens collective intelligence and a sense of belonging.

7. Repair vs. Punishment

Healthy norms

- Emphasize accountability alongside restoration
- Encourage apology, forgiveness, and learning
- Distinguish between harm and intent

Unhealthy norms

- Default to punishment or exclusion
- Avoid repair conversations
- Escalate conflict unnecessarily

Diagnostic signal: Punitive norms fracture relationships and reduce trust.

8. Subcultures as Assets vs. Threats

Healthy norms

- Allow subcultures to develop within shared values
- Learn from local innovation and experimentation

- Maintain dialogue between subcultures and the whole

Unhealthy norms

- Suppress the difference in the name of unity
- Treat deviation as disloyalty
- Allow fragmentation without shared values

Diagnostic signal: Flourishing balances coherence and diversity.

9. Collective Capacity vs. Anomie

Healthy norms

- Support cooperation and shared responsibility
- Help people feel oriented and connected
- Enable collective action in response to challenges

Unhealthy norms

- Leave people isolated, confused, or disengaged
- Normalize withdrawal or cynicism
- Fail to support collective problem-solving

Diagnostic signal: Anomie signals a breakdown in social support structures.

Using the Checklist

This checklist is not meant to label norms as good or bad in isolation. It helps identify:

- where norms are supporting flourishing,
- where they are generating unnecessary strain, and
- where thoughtful adjustment could improve collective life.

Healthy norms are not perfect or static. They are reflective, humane, and adaptable—providing structure without suffocation, and freedom without fragmentation.

Chapter 4

The Role of Cultural Touchpoints in a Flourishing Society

A SOCIETY'S VALUES and aspirations do not shape behavior on their own. They are translated into lived experience through cultural norms and a set of recurring encounters—formal and informal policies, practices, routines, and symbols—that establish, maintain, and change those norms. These encounters are **cultural touchpoints.**

Cultural touchpoints are powerful because they are frequent, often taken for granted, and emotionally instructive. They shape norms, signal priorities, and quietly influence attitudes and behavior over time. In a **flourishing society**, these touchpoints are deliberately aligned with flourishing values. In a strained or misaligned society, the same touchpoints may contradict stated values, normalize chronic stress, or reward behaviors that undermine dignity, connection, and well-being.

What follows is an exploration of key cultural touchpoints—each capable of either strengthening or weakening societal flourishing, depending on how it is designed and enacted.

Consider two organizations in the same industry, staffed by people of comparable talent, pursuing similar goals. In the first, meetings begin with a brief acknowledgment of recent wins and a candid word about current obstacles. Mistakes are discussed openly, celebrated as data. New hires are paired with mentors in their first week. Senior leaders are visibly curious rather than performatively confident. In the second, meetings are exercises in impression management. Errors are quietly buried. New hires spend months decoding unspoken rules. Leaders preach collaboration while competing for credit. Both organizations have written values that look nearly identical. The difference lies entirely in their touchpoints—the recurring practices and encounters through which those values are either lived or betrayed.

If Chapter 3 described the norms a flourishing society holds—the shared expectations that quietly govern behavior—this chapter maps the mechanisms through which those norms are made real. Touchpoints are where norms get enacted, tested, and either reinforced or undermined. Every time a community rewards one kind of behavior over another, every time a new member is welcomed or left to flounder, every time a leader acts with integrity under pressure or quietly abandons it, a touchpoint is doing its work.

No single touchpoint determines a culture. A community with generous resources but no investment in role modeling may still produce cynicism. One with inspiring narratives but chaotic roles may still exhaust its members. What matters is the cumulative weight—the degree to which touchpoints, taken together, tip the balance toward flourishing or away from it. Which touchpoints to focus on first depends on context: a community already motivated by financial rewards may need to start by redirecting those incentives, even as other touchpoints are elevated. A society that has lost trust in its institutions may need to begin with communication and accountability before anything else can be achieved. The goal is not a fixed order but a tipping point—enough aligned touchpoints working in the same direction for flourishing to become the path of least resistance.

1. Resource Commitment

Resources reveal what a society truly values. Funding, staffing, time, and attention communicate priorities more clearly than rhetoric.

- **When aligned:** Resources support health, learning, connection, and long-term well-being.
- **When misaligned:** Values are proclaimed but underfunded. People are expected to "care more" without adequate support, leading to burnout and cynicism.

A flourishing society understands that values without resources become moral burdens rather than shared commitments.

2. Built Environment

The physical and virtual spaces people inhabit shape behavior and emotional experience.

- **When aligned:** Spaces encourage interaction, accessibility, safety, and restoration. They support movement, connection, and inclusion.
- **When misaligned:** Environments are isolating, stressful, unsafe, or dehumanizing—requiring constant adaptation from those within them.

The built environment silently teaches people how much they matter and what the true priorities are.

3. Communication and Information

How information is shared influences trust, understanding, and engagement.

- **When aligned:** Communication is transparent, timely, and respectful. Complexity is acknowledged rather than obscured.
- **When misaligned:** Information is withheld, distorted, or overwhelming. Uncertainty breeds rumor, fear, and disengagement. A lack of feedback and information undermines shared values.

A flourishing society treats communication as a form of care, not a tool of control.

4. Rewards and Recognition

What is rewarded becomes normalized.

- **When aligned:** Recognition reinforces contribution, collaboration, kindness, learning, and sustainability. The rewards are seen as meaningful and adequate.
- **When misaligned:** Rewards favor overwork, competition, visibility over substance, or short-term gains at long-term cost. People learn to optimize for what is measured rather than what matters. In some contexts, financial rewards may temporarily sustain effort—but when they are the primary driver, they crowd out intrinsic motivation and signal that the culture does not trust people to care on their own.

A society cannot reward behavior that erodes well-being and expect flourishing to persist.

5. Goal Setting and Planning

Goals shape attention and effort.

- **When aligned:** Goals reflect flourishing values and long-term well-being. Planning balances ambition with realism and leaves room for adjustment. Complex changes are broken into achievable short and long-term goals.

- **When misaligned:** Goals are narrow, relentless, or detached from human capacity—creating chronic stress and moral injury. Actions feel haphazard and lacking forethought.

In a flourishing society, goals guide effort without eroding meaning or health.

6. Relationship Development

Social connection must be designed for, not assumed.

- **When aligned:** Touchpoints intentionally create opportunities for collaboration, dialogue, and mutual support. People form friendships and deep bonds through healthy, productive activities. There is abundant social capital.
- **When misaligned:** Work and civic life are structured in isolating ways, leaving relationships to chance. When bonding does occur, it can form around shared stress, complaint, or cynicism—which builds solidarity of a kind, but not the kind that supports flourishing. A society that bonds primarily through grievance will struggle to sustain collective effort.

A flourishing society recognizes that relationships are infrastructure.

7. Learning and Training

Learning touchpoints shape adaptability and growth.

- **When aligned:** Training builds skills for reflection, cooperation, and problem-solving across the lifespan. People feel confident in behaving in ways consistent with flourishing values.
- **When misaligned:** Learning is treated as remedial, optional, or purely technical—detached from lived challenges and

ethical reflection. People learn skills such as deception and control that run counter to flourishing.

A flourishing society treats learning as a shared capacity, not an individual deficit.

8. Role Modeling

People learn values by watching others, especially those with influence.

- **When aligned:** Leaders and peers model integrity, curiosity, kindness, and balance—especially under pressure. Role models demonstrate the benefit of living in accordance with flourishing values.
- **When misaligned:** Official values are contradicted by everyday behavior, eroding trust and increasing cynicism. There is a lack of positive leaders and peer models. The modeling that does exist runs against flourishing values.

Role modeling is one of the most efficient—and fragile—cultural touchpoints.

9. Pushback and Accountability

How a society responds to harm and deviation matters deeply.

- **When aligned:** Accountability emphasizes responsibility, repair, and learning. There is constructive pushback when someone behaves in ways inconsistent with the values of flourishing. Healthy and productive behavior is not met with such resistance.
- **When misaligned:** Responses default to blame, punishment, or avoidance—producing fear, resentment, or impunity.

A flourishing society holds people accountable without stripping dignity or collapsing trust.

10. Onboarding

Early experiences set expectations.

- **When aligned:** Those willing to adopt shared flourishing values are actively recruited and selected. New members are welcomed, oriented to flourishing values, and supported in belonging and contribution.
- **When misaligned:** People are left to "figure it out," reinforcing anxiety, exclusion, and unnecessary mistakes.

Onboarding reveals whether inclusion is intentional or merely symbolic.

11. Traditions and Symbols

Rituals and symbols communicate identity and continuity.

- **When aligned:** Traditions reinforce shared values, gratitude, and collective memory. The traditions and symbols convey a message consistent with flourishing values.
- **When misaligned:** Symbols become hollow, exclusionary, or nostalgic for a past that no longer serves.

A flourishing society periodically reexamines its symbols to ensure they continue to unify and strengthen a sense of belonging.

12. Story and Narrative

The stories a society tells shape meaning and possibility.

- **When aligned:** Narratives emphasize agency, learning, care, and shared responsibility. Stories of past actions and future aspirations embody flourishing values.
- **When misaligned:** Stories normalize exploitation, inevitability, scapegoating, or zero-sum thinking.

Narratives quietly train people in what to expect from life together—and what they believe is possible.

13. Roles and Responsibilities

Clarity of roles reduces stress and conflict.

- **When aligned:** Responsibilities are realistic, shared, and well-defined. Care work is acknowledged and supported.
- **When misaligned:** Roles are ambiguous, overloaded, or unfairly distributed, producing chronic role strain.

A flourishing society avoids organizing life in ways that require ongoing overload as the price of participation.

14. Laws and Policies

Formal rules establish the outer boundaries of culture.

- **When aligned:** Laws protect dignity, equity, safety, and long-term well-being. They are not so restrictive as to undermine personal freedoms and the well-being of subcultures.
- **When misaligned:** Policies incentivize harm, neglect vulnerability, or prioritize efficiency over humanity. Favoritism and unequal justice undermine the flourishing culture.

Laws cannot create flourishing alone, but they can either protect it or repeatedly undermine it.

Aligning Touchpoints with a Flourishing Society

Cultural touchpoints are not neutral. They are design choices—often inherited, sometimes invisible, but always influential. A flourishing society periodically examines these touchpoints to ask:

- What behaviors are we reinforcing?
- What attitudes are we normalizing?
- What experiences are we making routine?

When touchpoints align with a flourishing culture, they reduce the psychological effort required to live well together. When they do not, individuals are left to compensate privately for systemic misalignment.

A flourishing society takes this alignment seriously—not as a one-time reform but as an ongoing practice of stewardship. In doing so, it transforms culture from an accidental inheritance into a deliberate support for dignity, well-being, and collective capacity.

Diagnostic Checklist: Cultural Touchpoints in a Flourishing Society

Cultural touchpoints are the repeated policies, practices, and experiences through which people encounter a culture. Use this checklist to assess which touchpoints are working, which are misaligned, and where the greatest leverage for change may lie. Look for patterns over time, not isolated incidents. The questions below are diagnostic, not prescriptive—the goal is clarity about where you are, as the foundation for deciding where to focus.

1. Resource Commitment

What do time, money, and attention actually support?

- Are resources allocated to health, learning, connection, and prevention?
- Do budgets and staffing match stated priorities?
- Is caring work adequately supported?
- Are people expected to compensate personally for underfunded values?

Warning sign: Values are praised rhetorically but starved of material support.

2. Built Environment

What do spaces invite people to do and feel?

- Do physical and virtual spaces encourage interaction and inclusion?
- Are environments accessible, safe, and humane?
- Do spaces reduce stress—or amplify it?
- Do people feel respected by the environments they inhabit?

Warning sign: People must constantly adapt to spaces that are depleting or alienating.

3. Communication and Information

How is information shared and interpreted?

- Is communication transparent, timely, and understandable?
- Are people given the information and feedback they need to accomplish their goals?
- Are uncertainty and complexity acknowledged?
- Do people trust what they are told?
- Is information used to orient—or to control?

Warning sign: Confusion, rumor, and distrust dominate.

4. Rewards and Recognition

What behavior is reinforced?

- Are collaboration, kindness, learning, and sustainability recognized?
- Is overwork or competition implicitly rewarded?

- Are contributions acknowledged broadly and fairly?
- Do recognition systems reflect shared values?

Warning sign: Harmful behaviors are incentivized despite stated values.

5. Goal Setting and Planning

Do goals guide without overwhelming?

- Are goals aligned with human capacity and long-term well-being?
- Do plans include space for learning and adjustment?
- Are trade-offs discussed openly?
- Do goals create meaning—or constant pressure?

Warning sign: Chronic urgency and moral exhaustion.

6. Relationship Development

Are relationships intentionally supported?

- Are there built-in opportunities for connection and collaboration?
- Is mutual support normalized?
- Are people isolated by design?
- Are friendships and other relationships formed around positive practices?

Warning sign: Social connection is left to chance.

7. Learning and Training

Is growth supported across the lifespan?

- Do learning opportunities build reflective and relational skills?

- Is learning proactive rather than remedial?
- Are mistakes treated as learning opportunities?
- Do people feel safe admitting uncertainty?

Warning sign: Learning is stigmatized or narrowly technical.

8. Role Modeling

What behaviors are demonstrated by influential people?

- Do leaders and peers model flourishing values?
- Is kindness visible in moments of stress?
- Are learning and accountability modeled?
- Are contradictions noticed and addressed?

Warning sign: "Do as I say, not as I do" culture.

9. Pushback and Accountability

How does the system respond to harm or deviation?

- Is accountability paired with dignity and repair?
- Are boundaries clear and fair?
- Is constructive behavior protected rather than penalized?
- Are problems addressed—or avoided?

Warning sign: Fear, impunity, or punitive escalation.

10. Onboarding

What do newcomers learn first?

- Does the recruitment and selection process acknowledge the goal of flourishing?
- Are new members welcomed and oriented to shared flourishing values?
- Are norms explained rather than assumed?

- Is belonging intentional?
- Are people left to sink or swim?

Warning sign: Early anxiety and exclusion.

11. Traditions and Symbols

What is celebrated and remembered?

- Do rituals reinforce shared values and inclusion?
- Are symbols meaningful and current?
- Are traditions periodically re-examined?
- Do symbols unite—or divide?

Warning sign: Empty or exclusionary rituals.

12. Story and Narrative

What stories shape expectations?

- Do our stories sufficiently explain why we aspire to flourish?
- Do narratives emphasize agency, learning, and care?
- Are challenges framed as solvable?
- Are people portrayed as disposable or replaceable?
- Does the story invite participation—or resignation?

Warning sign: Fatalism or an inability to tell a story that links flourishing to our own story.

13. Roles and Responsibilities

Is responsibility clear and fair?

- Are roles well-defined and realistic?
- Is care work acknowledged and shared?
- Are responsibilities distributed equitably?
- Do role expectations support well-being?

Warning sign: Chronic role strain and ambiguity.

14. Laws and Policies

What behavior is formally permitted or constrained?

- Do laws protect dignity, equity, and long-term well-being?
- Are unintended consequences examined?
- Do policies reduce harm—or normalize it?
- Are rules enforced fairly?
- Do unnecessary rules and laws undermine expression and diversity?

Warning sign: Legal structures incentivize distress or exploitation.

Integrative Questions

How do the touchpoints work together?

- Do touchpoints reinforce flourishing values consistently?
- Do they strengthen a sense of community, shared vision, and positive outlook?
- Do they reduce the effort required to live well together?
- Where do people compensate personally for systemic misalignment?
- Are there contradictions between touchpoints—where one sends a message that another undermines? (For example: a generous parental leave policy that no one uses because role modeling signals it would be career-limiting.)
- Given this community's particular history and current readiness, which two or three touchpoints, if aligned now, would most plausibly shift the overall balance toward flourishing?

Using the Checklist

This checklist is not about perfection. It is about **alignment.** Cultural touchpoints shape behavior, whether or not we address them. A flourishing society makes touchpoints visible, examines their impact, and intentionally adjusts them.

When touchpoints align with shared values of flourishing, people feel supported rather than strained, oriented rather than confused, and engaged rather than resigned. That alignment is one of the clearest—and most practical—markers of societal flourishing.

Chapter 5

The Role of Peer Support in a Flourishing Society

A FLOURISHING SOCIETY does not rely solely on professionals, institutions, or formal systems to support well-being. It depends just as deeply on the everyday presence of peers—coworkers, neighbors, friends, and family—who form the living fabric of daily life. These peer relationships create conditions in which people feel seen, supported, and capable of navigating both everyday stress and extraordinary challenges.

In a flourishing society, mutual support is neither accidental nor heroic. It is expected, learned, and valued. People recognize that well-being is sustained not only by services and policies but also by relationships that offer reassurance, practical help, encouragement, and connection.

Peer Support as Social Infrastructure

Peer relationships serve as social infrastructure, quietly supporting individuals long before problems escalate into crises. A colleague notices when someone is overwhelmed. A neighbor checks in after an illness. Friends make space for honest conversation. Families share responsibility rather than leaving individuals to cope alone.

These interactions are not treated as intrusions or burdens. They are part of what it means to live well together. In a flourishing society, people do not wait for formal authority or professional intervention to provide care, nor do they try to replace professional help when it is needed. Instead, peer support serves as a bridge—strengthening everyday resilience and, when appropriate, connecting people to additional resources.

That bridge metaphor matters. Peer support and professional infrastructure are not substitutes for each other—they are complementary. A society that invests heavily in peer networks while defunding mental health services, social work, or community health is not building a flourishing system; it is offloading institutional responsibility onto informal relationships. Conversely, a society that relies entirely on professionals while eroding the everyday connections between people will find that formal systems alone cannot sustain well-being at scale. The goal is both robust professional support and robust peer support, each reinforcing the other.

What this looks like in practice can be seen in communities that have deliberately woven peer support into their fabric. In some Scandinavian workplaces, for example, structured peer check-ins are built into the working week—a norm negotiated and maintained by teams themselves. New employees are paired with experienced colleagues not only for technical onboarding but for social integration. Difficult conversations about workload and stress are normalized rather than stigmatized. The result is not the elimination of difficulty, but the reduction of the isolation that makes difficulty unbearable. These practices did not emerge from personality; they were designed, modeled by leaders, and sustained through the kinds of touchpoints described in the previous chapter. They demonstrate that, when properly cultivated, peer support can shift from an accidental feature of lucky teams to a reliable feature of intentional cultures.

None of this happens automatically. Several forces work against it. Time pressure compresses the moments in which care can be offered and received. Geographic mobility erodes the long-term relationships that make mutual support feel natural. Cultural norms of self-sufficiency—particularly strong in individualistic societies—make it feel risky to ask for help and awkward to offer it. Digital communication creates a simulacrum of connection without always sustaining it: people may have hundreds of contacts and still feel profoundly alone. And economic precarity makes mutual care harder to sustain, not because people care less but because exhaustion and scarcity leave less to give. A flourishing society does not look away from these obstacles. It names them, designs against them, and builds the cultural and structural conditions in which peer support can take root despite them.

Comfort with Giving and Receiving Support

One measure of societal flourishing is how readily people both offer and accept support. In strained cultures, people hesitate to help for fear of overstepping and to receive help for fear of appearing weak. In a flourishing society, these anxieties are reduced by shared norms and relational skills.

People learn how to:

- notice signs of stress or withdrawal,
- ask supportive questions without interrogation,

- listen without immediately fixing or judging,
- offer help without assuming control, and
- respect boundaries while remaining present.

Just as importantly, people learn that seeking support is not a failure of independence but a normal expression of interdependence. This mutual comfort strengthens trust and reduces isolation.

Learning the Skills of Peer Support

Peer support in a flourishing society is not left to chance or personality alone. It is cultivated intentionally. People learn basic skills for supporting one another in families, schools, workplaces, and communities.

These skills include:

- communicating empathy and encouragement,
- distinguishing between emotional support and problem-solving,
- recognizing when a situation exceeds one's role, and
- helping someone access professional or community resources when needed.

By normalizing these skills, a flourishing society prevents the common extremes of emotional neglect on the one hand and untrained overreach on the other. Peer support becomes reliable, appropriate, and sustainable.

Instrumental and Emotional Support

Healthy peer relationships provide instrumental and emotional support, depending on the situation.

Instrumental support includes practical help—such as sharing information, adjusting workloads, providing transportation, assisting with tasks, or coordinating resources.

Emotional support includes listening, reassurance, validation, humor, and simple presence during difficult moments.

In a flourishing society, people are attentive to the support that is actually needed. They do not assume that emotional pain always requires solutions or that practical problems must be faced alone. This flexibility makes support more effective and less draining for everyone involved.

Communication That Strengthens Peer Support

Peer support is reinforced by how people speak to one another. In a flourishing society, communication norms favor respectful, encouraging, and constructive language. This does not mean avoiding difficult conversations or pretending everything is fine. It means addressing challenges without shaming, dismissing, or being unnecessarily harsh.

Constructive communication includes:

- expressing appreciation and gratitude,
- acknowledging effort as well as outcomes,
- offering feedback in ways that preserve dignity, and
- recognizing one another's contributions openly.

Such communication strengthens morale, deepens connections, and makes it easier to seek help when needed.

Feeling Appreciated and Valued

Peer relationships are a primary source of recognition and belonging. In a flourishing society, people regularly experience appreciation—not only for exceptional achievements but also for everyday contributions.

Feeling appreciated:

- reinforces a sense of purpose,
- reduces burnout, and
- increases willingness to support others in return.

This reciprocal recognition creates a positive cycle: people who feel valued are more likely to notice and value others.

Shared Opportunity and Shared Responsibility

In a flourishing society, peer support is understood as both an opportunity and a responsibility. It is an opportunity to strengthen relationships, contribute to collective well-being, and find meaning in mutual care. It is a responsibility because social bonds do not sustain themselves automatically; they require attention, effort, and cultural reinforcement.

Importantly, this responsibility is shared rather than imposed on a few. Care is not relegated to the most compassionate individuals or overburdened helpers. Instead, norms, skills, and expectations distribute support work broadly and realistically.

In practice, care work is rarely distributed equitably. Across most cultures, women carry a disproportionate share of emotional labor—the work of noticing others' distress, managing relational tension, and providing comfort. Informal caregivers, often family members supporting aging parents or relatives with illness or disability, absorb enormous burdens with minimal recognition or relief. And within communities, the most empathic individuals frequently become de facto support hubs, absorbing others' distress until they burn out. A flourishing society sees these patterns clearly. It actively redistributes care through shared norms, structured practices, and formal recognition of informal caregiving—not as a favor to those who currently carry too much but as a basic condition of sustainable collective life.

Peers and Collective Flourishing

When peer support networks are strong, societies become more resilient. Stress is noticed earlier. Problems are addressed before they escalate. People remain engaged rather than withdrawing in silence. The collective capacity to cope, adapt, and learn together is strengthened.

In this sense, peer support is not merely a kindness—it is a core component of collective flourishing. A society where people routinely feel appreciated, supported, and connected can face uncertainty without fragmenting.

A flourishing society recognizes this and acts on it deliberately. It cultivates peer support through the norms described in Chapter 3—shared expectations that make mutual care feel normal rather than exceptional—and through the touchpoints described in Chapter 4: the practices, environments, and interactions that either invite connection or foreclose it. When those norms and touchpoints are aligned, peer support stops being a matter of individual personality or goodwill and becomes a reliable feature of collective life. The positive cycle deepens: people who feel genuinely valued become more attentive to others; communities where care is visible become easier to trust; and societies with high trust become better able to navigate difficulties together. How people care for one another in ordinary moments ultimately determines whether life together is merely bearable or genuinely sustaining.

Diagnostic Questions: Peer Support in a Flourishing Society

These questions help assess whether peer relationships are functioning as a source of mutual support, resilience, and flourishing—or whether isolation, avoidance, or overreliance on formal systems has taken hold.

1. Availability of Peer Support

Are supportive relationships present and accessible in daily life?

- Do people feel they have someone to turn to in ordinary moments of stress?
- Are coworkers, neighbors, friends, or family members generally attentive to one another?
- Is checking in on others a common and accepted practice?
- Are people noticed when they are struggling—or do difficulties often go unseen?

Diagnostic signal: When people routinely feel invisible or alone, peer networks are not functioning.

2. Comfort With Giving and Receiving Support

Is mutual support emotionally safe and socially acceptable?

- Do people feel comfortable offering help without fear of overstepping?
- Do people feel comfortable accepting help without shame or embarrassment?
- Are vulnerability and honesty met with respect?
- Is independence defined in a way that allows interdependence?

Diagnostic signal: Cultures that equate needing help with weakness discourage flourishing peer support.

3. Skills for Providing Appropriate Support

Do peers know how to support one another well?

- Do people know how to listen without rushing to fix?
- Can peers distinguish between emotional support and problem-solving?

- Are boundaries respected?
- Do people know when and how to help someone access additional assistance?

Diagnostic signal: Without basic relational skills, good intentions can result in avoidance or missteps.

4. Instrumental Support

Is practical help available when needed?

- Do people help one another with tasks, information, or coordination?
- Are workloads or responsibilities adjusted when someone is under strain?
- Do systems make it easy for peers to assist one another?
- Is asking for practical help normalized?

Diagnostic signal: When people are left to manage practical challenges on their own, stress compounds unnecessarily.

5. Emotional Support

Is emotional presence valued and practiced?

- Are people given space to express frustration, sadness, or uncertainty?
- Do peers respond with empathy rather than dismissal or minimization?
- Is humor used to uplift rather than deflect or demean?
- Are difficult emotions tolerated without pressure to "move on" too quickly?

Diagnostic signal: Emotional neglect erodes trust even when practical help is present.

6. Uplifting Communication

Does everyday communication strengthen morale and connection?

- Do people regularly express appreciation and gratitude?
- Is feedback delivered in ways that preserve dignity?
- Are strengths and efforts acknowledged openly?
- Does language tend to build people up rather than wear them down?

Diagnostic signal: Consistently harsh or indifferent communication patterns undermine peer-based flourishing.

7. Reciprocity and Shared Responsibility

Is support mutual rather than one-sided?

- Is the responsibility for care broadly shared?
- Are helpers supported as well?
- Do people experience both giving and receiving support over time?
- Is caregiving recognized rather than taken for granted?

Diagnostic signal: When support falls to a few, burnout and resentment follow.

8. Connection to Additional Resources

Do peer networks link people to help further when needed?

- Do peers know what resources are available?
- Are referrals to professional or community support made thoughtfully?
- Is seeking additional help framed as wise rather than as failure?
- Do peers remain supportive even when professionals become involved?

Diagnostic signal: Isolation from resources increases risk during periods of strain.

9. Inclusion and Belonging

Do peer relationships foster a sense of belonging among diverse individuals?

- Are people with different abilities, backgrounds, or communication styles included?
- Are newcomers welcomed and oriented?
- Do social networks avoid cliques that exclude or marginalize?
- Are differences handled with curiosity rather than judgment?

Diagnostic signal: Exclusion weakens collective resilience and capacity.

10. Impact on Collective Flourishing

Do peer relationships reduce distress and strengthen resilience?

- Do people feel appreciated and valued?
- Is stress noticed and addressed early?
- Are people more likely to stay engaged during difficulty?
- Do peer relationships support hope, agency, and trust?

Diagnostic signal: Strong peer support is a powerful indicator of societal flourishing.

Using the Diagnostic

These questions are not meant to measure perfection but capacity. Healthy peer support is neither constant nor effortless—it is cultivated, uneven at times, and strengthened through attention and practice.

A flourishing society recognizes that peer support is not optional. It is a shared opportunity and responsibility—one of the most powerful ways people sustain one another and safeguard collective well-being.

Chapter 6

The Role of Leadership Support in a Flourishing Society

A FLOURISHING SOCIETY does not emerge by accident. It is shaped, sustained, and renewed through leadership—formal and informal, visible and quiet—exercised across every domain of life. In this sense, leadership is not confined to titles or positions of authority. It includes managers and policymakers, peer leaders, parents, educators, community organizers, and anyone whose actions influence shared direction and norms.

In a flourishing society, leadership is understood less as control and more as stewardship: the responsibility for the social conditions that enable people and communities to thrive.

Flourishing, as used throughout this book, refers to a condition in which people can live with dignity, develop their capacities, maintain meaningful relationships, and participate in communities they care about. It is not merely the absence of harm or the satisfaction of basic needs but the presence of conditions that make a genuinely good life possible. Leadership matters to flourishing because those conditions are never given—they must be actively built and maintained.

Leadership as a Distributed Function

Flourishing societies recognize that leadership is distributed rather than centralized. While formal leaders play critical roles in setting policy and allocating resources, informal leaders shape culture through daily actions—how meetings are run, how conflict is handled, how effort is recognized, and how people are treated when they struggle.

Peer leaders, in particular, play a vital role. They translate values into practice on the ground, model supportive behavior, and often set the emotional tone of groups. In a flourishing society, these informal leadership roles are acknowledged, supported, and respected rather than ignored or exploited.

Leadership shows up wherever people coordinate action: in workplaces, households, schools, neighborhoods, civic groups, and governments. The cumulative effect of leadership across these settings helps determine whether society feels coherent or chaotic, hopeful or depleted—and whether flourishing is realistic or merely aspirational.

Consider a mid-sized school where the principal has articulated a clear commitment to student well-being. That commitment matters, but its impact depends far more on how a veteran teacher greets struggling students in the morning, how a department head responds when a colleague makes a mistake, and how a group of students treats an isolated peer. None of these people holds formal authority over the others. Yet together they determine whether the school's stated values are lived or merely displayed. In a flourishing society, this kind of distributed leadership is not an accident—it is cultivated.

Creating and Communicating a Vision

One of the most important functions of leadership in a flourishing society is to create and communicate a shared vision. Leaders help answer fundamental questions:

- What kind of society are we trying to build?
- Why does it matter?
- How does our daily work contribute to that aim?

A compelling vision of a flourishing society clarifies what is valued—productive work, health, joy, kindness, learning, and connection—and why these matter not only morally but also psychologically and practically. It helps people look beyond short-term pressures and understand how their efforts fit into a larger story.

Crucially, vision is not a slogan. It must be revisited, refined, and embodied. Leaders keep it alive by referencing it in decisions, using it to guide trade-offs, and inviting others to help shape it as conditions evolve.

It's important to ask not only how vision succeeds but also how it fails—because failure is more common. A vision often fails to take hold, not because it is poorly communicated but because of a lack of follow-through and alignment with cultural touchpoints. Belief diminishes when declared priorities conflict with actual behavior: for example, when a community organization states that every voice matters but decisions are made without consultation; or when a government agency promotes a vision of dignity and inclusion while staff face ongoing disrespect from their managers. In these situations, the vision doesn't simply disappear—it inverts. It becomes a sign of hypocrisy, making people more cynical than they would have been without it. This is a widespread and under-acknowledged pattern in organizational and civic life. Leaders who genuinely value their vision must therefore consider credibility as essential. Before asking people to believe in a shared future, they need to honestly assess whether current conditions support that belief—and confront the truth of what they find.

Leading by Example

Leadership in a flourishing society is visible in behavior. Leaders act as role models for the values they espouse. They demonstrate:

- respect and kindness in communication,
- openness to learning and feedback,
- accountability for mistakes, and
- care for their own well-being and that of others.

When leaders model healthy norms, they make it psychologically safer for others to do the same. When they fail to do so, even the most eloquent statements of values lose credibility.

Leading by example is especially important for informal leaders. Everyday actions—listening attentively, acknowledging effort, setting boundaries, and expressing appreciation—often have more influence on culture than formal directives.

A neighborhood association coordinator who responds to a heated disagreement by slowing down, asking clarifying questions, and naming what she has heard models something more powerful than any written policy on respectful dialogue. A senior nurse who visibly takes a break during a long shift and encourages colleagues to do the same normalizes sustainable effort in a way that no wellness initiative can replicate. These are small acts, but their cumulative effect on culture is significant. Modeling works precisely because it bypasses the skepticism that formal messaging often triggers. When people see values enacted rather than announced, they become more likely to enact them in turn.

Aligning Policies, Practices, and Norms

A critical leadership responsibility is alignment. In a flourishing society, leaders work to ensure:

- formal policies reflect stated values,
- informal practices reinforce those policies, and
- incentives do not undermine well-being or trust.

Misalignment is one of the most common sources of strain. When organizations claim to value health yet reward overwork, or claim to value learning yet punish mistakes, people become cynical and disengaged.

Leaders support flourishing by examining how systems function—how performance is measured, decisions are made, and power is exercised—and by adjusting them so that daily experience better reflects human needs and shared priorities.

When Formal and Informal Leadership Conflict

Because leadership is distributed, it is not always unified. Formal and informal leaders sometimes point in opposite directions, and this tension is one of the most practical challenges a flourishing society must navigate.

Consider a civic organization whose executive director has introduced a new initiative around transparency and shared decision-making. The formal structure supports it. But a long-tenured program manager—respected, well connected, informally influential—is skeptical. She does not openly sabotage the initiative. Instead, she expresses doubt in small ways: an eye roll in a meeting, a comment to a colleague that signals the change is performative, a delay in implementing the new process within her team. Because she is trusted, her skepticism spreads. The formal initiative loses momentum not because it was poorly designed but because informal leadership was running a different program.

This scenario illustrates why distributing leadership is not enough. Informal leaders must be brought into genuine dialogue about direction and change—not simply informed of decisions made elsewhere. When formal leaders understand that informal leaders are essential partners rather than obstacles or subordinates, and when informal leaders take their influence on collective capacity seriously, the two forms of leadership can reinforce rather than undermine each other. A flourishing society does not expect perfect agreement among its members. It expects honest engagement.

There are also cases in which informal leadership carries the organization's values more faithfully than formal leadership does—where peer leaders maintain care and dignity under conditions that formal structures have neglected or eroded. In those situations, informal leadership is not a source of resistance; it is a source of resilience. Recognizing the difference matters enormously for how formal leaders respond.

Removing Barriers and Creating Conditions

Leadership support in a flourishing society goes beyond encouragement. It includes the practical work of removing barriers that prevent people from fully contributing or supporting one another.

This may involve:

- redesigning workflows that create unnecessary stress,
- addressing inequities in access to resources,
- clarifying roles and expectations, or
- reducing bureaucratic friction that drains energy and morale.

By shaping conditions rather than blaming individuals, leaders reinforce the idea that well-being and effectiveness are shared responsibilities—and that flourishing is built into systems, not demanded as private resilience.

Tracking and Celebrating Progress

Flourishing societies focus on what is improving—not only on what is failing. Leaders play a key role in tracking progress toward shared goals and celebrating success in meaningful ways.

This includes:

- recognizing individual and collective contributions,
- highlighting improvements in well-being, cooperation, or learning, and
- making progress visible to sustain motivation and realistic hope.

In this sense, celebration is not superficial. It reinforces values, strengthens connections, and reminds people that change is possible.

What Leaders Must Avoid

Leadership can also undermine flourishing. Certain patterns consistently erode trust and well-being, regardless of context.

Dishonesty is among the most corrosive. This includes not only outright deception but the subtler forms: spin that obscures difficult realities, denial of plainly visible problems, and the selective withholding of information that people need to understand their situation. Dishonesty rapidly damages trust, and once trust is lost, it is difficult to restore. People who feel misled tend to disengage—not just from the leader who misled them but from shared projects and institutions more broadly. A single act of institutional dishonesty can take years to repair.

Closely related is the absence of empathy—especially during stress or uncertainty, when the need for it is highest. Leaders who project indifference during difficult periods send a powerful message about whose experience matters. They do not need to manufacture warmth they do not feel; they do need to develop the capacity to acknowledge what others are going through, and to let that acknowledgment inform their decisions.

The failure to give constructive feedback is a quieter form of harm, but it is real. When people lack honest information about how their work is landing or how they might grow, they are left to fill the gap with assumptions—often self-critical, often inaccurate. Leaders sometimes avoid feedback because they fear conflict or wish to protect relationships. In practice, this avoidance often does more damage than the difficult conversation would have.

Disregard for the future—prioritizing short-term gains at the expense of long-term well-being, sustainability, or trust—is a structural failure that may not be visible in its early stages. Leaders who consistently choose the convenient over the durable gradually deplete the conditions that make flourishing possible. By the time the consequences are clear, the work of repair is far more costly than prevention would have been. And blame-based responses that treat systemic failures as individual shortcomings compound the damage by discouraging learning and reinforcing the fear that mistakes are dangerous rather than instructive.

What these patterns share is that they are recognizable long before their worst effects materialize. People generally know when they are being misled, dismissed, or set up to fail. The behaviors listed above do not usually surprise those who experience them—they confirm what was already suspected. This is why avoiding them is not simply a matter of ethical conduct, though it is that. It is a matter of institutional realism. Communities and organizations that tolerate these patterns consistently discover that the cost is borne not by those who exhibit them but by everyone else.

Leadership and Collective Flourishing

Ultimately, leadership support is among the strongest predictors of collective well-being and collective capacity. When leadership is thoughtful, humane, and aligned with shared values, people feel safer, more engaged, and more capable of working together. When leadership is inconsistent, self-serving, or dismissive, strain spreads quickly.

A flourishing society does not expect leaders to be perfect. It expects them to be responsible—to learn, listen, correct course, and keep the future in view. At its best, leadership helps people believe that their efforts matter and that the society they are building together is worth caring about.

In this way, leadership support becomes not merely a function of authority but a shared social practice—one that sustains flourishing across institutions, communities, and generations.

Diagnostic Questions: Leadership Support in a Flourishing Society

These questions help assess whether formal and informal leadership is strengthening—or unintentionally undermining—the conditions for well-being, dignity, learning, and collective capacity. Patterns over time matter more than isolated behaviors.

1. Presence of Leadership at Multiple Levels

Is leadership distributed and visible across the system?

- Are leadership roles exercised beyond formal titles?
- Do peer leaders feel empowered to influence norms and practices?

- Are leadership responsibilities shared rather than concentrated in a few roles?
- Do people know who to turn to for guidance and support?

Diagnostic signal: When leadership is absent, unclear, or overly centralized, confusion and disengagement increase.

2. Clarity of Vision

Do leaders articulate a clear, humane vision of what they are building?

- Is there a shared understanding of what a flourishing system looks like?
- Do leaders explain why the vision matters—not just what to do?
- Is the vision referenced in decisions, trade-offs, and priorities?
- Are people invited to refine and help carry the vision forward?

Diagnostic signal: Without vision, effort fragments, and meaning erodes.

3. Modeling of Values

Do leaders embody the values they promote?

- Do leaders demonstrate kindness, respect, and integrity in daily interactions?
- Are leaders open about learning, mistakes, and growth?
- Do leaders model healthy boundaries and sustainable effort?
- Is leadership behavior consistent under stress?

Diagnostic signal: When leaders' actions contradict stated values, trust declines rapidly.

4. Alignment of Touch Points

Do leaders take the initiative to align formal and informal cultural influences with flourishing values?

- Do they work to align formal policies?
- Do leaders work to align informal influences?
- Are contradictions noticed and addressed?

Diagnostic signal: Leaders are passive or dismissive of the day-to-day influences within their control.

5. Support for Learning and Feedback

Do leaders create conditions for growth and adaptation?

- Is constructive feedback provided regularly and respectfully?
- Are questions and dissent welcomed?
- Do leaders adjust course in response to new information?
- Is learning framed as a collective responsibility?

Diagnostic signal: Fear of feedback or punishment signals a decline in collective capacity.

6. Removal of Barriers

Do leaders actively reduce obstacles that impede well-being and effectiveness?

- Are unnecessary stressors identified and addressed?
- Do leaders examine system design rather than blaming individuals?
- Are inequities acknowledged and acted upon?
- Do leaders advocate for resources and structural change when needed?

Diagnostic signal: When barriers persist unchallenged, leadership credibility erodes.

7. Support for Peer and Relational Infrastructure

Do leaders strengthen relationships and mutual support?

- Are peer support efforts recognized and encouraged?
- Do leaders protect time and space for connection?
- Are caregivers and informal leaders supported rather than exploited?
- Do leaders notice relational strain and intervene constructively?

Diagnostic signal: Neglect of relationships weakens resilience and collective flourishing.

8. Recognition and Celebration

Do leaders notice and reinforce progress?

- Are contributions acknowledged regularly?
- Are improvements in well-being, cooperation, or learning celebrated?
- Do leaders highlight collective successes rather than just individual performance?
- Is appreciation authentic and specific?

Diagnostic signal: Absence of recognition leads to disengagement and fatigue.

9. Ethical Conduct and Trustworthiness

Do leaders act with honesty and moral responsibility?

- Is information shared transparently?
- Are difficult truths addressed rather than avoided?
- Do leaders accept responsibility for mistakes?
- Is trust repaired when it is damaged?

Diagnostic signal: Dishonesty corrodes collective well-being and trust.

10. Future Orientation and Stewardship

Do leaders keep the long term in view?

- Are decisions evaluated for long-term human and social impact?
- Do leaders consider sustainability, intergenerational effects, and well-being?
- Is short-term pressure balanced against enduring values?
- Do leaders speak explicitly about the future they are helping to shape?

Diagnostic signal: Disregard for future signals, moral and psychological short-sightedness.

11. What Leaders Avoid

Are harmful leadership patterns actively discouraged?

- Is blame replaced with responsibility and repair?
- Is power exercised with care rather than intimidation?
- Are empathy and kindness treated as strengths rather than liabilities?
- Are people given clarity rather than silence or mixed messages?

Diagnostic signal: Toxic leadership behaviors rapidly spread strain and disengagement.

Integrative Questions

What is the overall impact of leadership on collective flourishing?

- Do people feel supported, oriented, and valued?
- Is there a realistic hope that effort leads to improvement?

- Do people remain engaged during difficulty?
- Can the system learn and adapt without waiting for a crisis to occur?

Using the Diagnostic

This diagnostic is not about identifying "good" or "bad" leaders. It is about assessing whether leadership functions are fulfilled in ways that support a flourishing society.

Healthy leadership is not flawless. It is reflective, accountable, and future-oriented—and it recognizes that leadership is a shared responsibility. When leadership at all levels reinforces dignity, learning, connection, and long-term stewardship, flourishing becomes more than an aspiration. It becomes a lived, renewable reality.

Chapter 7

The Role of Social Climate in a Flourishing Society

EVERY SOCIETY HAS a **social climate**—a pervasive, felt quality of daily life that shapes how people experience belonging, purpose, and possibility. Social climate is related to, but distinct from, culture and morale. Culture refers to the enduring values, beliefs, and practices of a group—its identity over time. Social climate is integral to culture, along with other elements such as values, norms, peer support, and touchpoints. Morale refers to the confidence and motivation of individuals within a group at a given moment. Social climate is something different: the ambient quality of collective life as experienced day to day. It is not what a community believes or how its members feel individually but how it feels to be in that community—the emotional and relational texture of shared existence. It can shift faster than culture and is more structural than morale, making it both highly influential and meaningfully responsive to intentional effort. In a flourishing society, the social climate is characterized by three reinforcing elements: **a sense of community, a shared vision, and a positive outlook**. Together, these create conditions in which people can engage meaningfully with one another and with the future. When they are present, society feels coherent and capable. When they are noticeably absent, well-being and effectiveness suffer—often in predictable and preventable ways.

Social Climate as a Determinant of Flourishing

Social climate shapes how people interpret their experiences. It influences whether stress is perceived as manageable or overwhelming, whether effort is perceived as worthwhile or futile, and whether challenges elicit cooperation or withdrawal. In an unhealthy social climate, individuals may appear functional on the surface while experiencing chronic strain beneath it.

A degraded social climate often produces:

- heightened anxiety and cynicism,
- disengagement and reduced productivity,
- increased conflict or social withdrawal, and
- rising levels of burnout and distress.

These outcomes are frequently misattributed to individual weakness or lack of motivation. In a flourishing society, they are recognized as signals that the social environment itself needs attention and renewal.

Sense of Community: Belonging and Mutual Responsibility

A sense of community reflects the degree to which people feel they belong, are valued, and are part of something larger than themselves. It is built through trust, familiarity, and shared experience.

Where a sense of community is strong, people:

- care for one another in times of need,
- stay current on one another's activities and interests,
- have come to know one another well,
- trust one another,
- feel comfortable saying what is on their minds, and
- look forward to a future together.

Where it is weak or absent, people become isolated, guarded, and less willing to contribute. Loneliness increases—even in crowded settings—and collaboration becomes a burden.

The difference is palpable. Consider two housing developments built in the same year in the same city. In one, residents know their neighbors' names, keep an eye on one another's property, and gather occasionally around a shared green. When a family faces hardship, meals appear. Conflict arises sometimes, but it is addressed rather than left to fester. In the other development, residents pass each other in silence. A newcomer moves in and meets no one for months. When something goes wrong, people deal with it alone or not at all. The physical infrastructure is identical. The social climate is completely different—and so are the mental health outcomes, the crime rates, and the residents' sense that they can shape their own lives. Neither development chose its climate consciously. But both could.

Strengthening a Sense of Community

Actions that support this dimension include:

- Creating regular opportunities for connection and shared experience, such as shared meals, community rituals, or cross-functional projects that require genuine collaboration rather than parallel work

- Establishing norms of inclusion and respect
- Recognizing contributions broadly and consistently, attending especially to contributions that are easily overlooked—the person who quietly holds things together, the peer who checks in on struggling colleagues, the newcomer whose perspective changed a decision
- Designing physical and social spaces that encourage interaction rather than fragmentation

A flourishing society understands that community does not emerge spontaneously; it must be intentionally cultivated. This cultivation is less about programs and more about consistent, low-cost practices: greeting people by name, asking genuine questions, noticing absence, repairing ruptures when they occur. The accumulation of these small acts is what community is actually made of.

Shared Vision: Direction and Meaning

A shared vision provides direction. It answers the question: *Where are we trying to go together, and why does it matter?* This vision need not be rigid or unanimous, but it must be sufficiently clear to guide decisions and sustain effort.

What is less often recognized is how directly a shared vision shapes the texture of daily interaction—not just institutional decisions. When people understand where they are headed together and why it matters, ordinary exchanges take on a different character. A difficult conversation at work becomes easier to have when both parties know they share an underlying goal. A disagreement in a community meeting stays productive when participants feel aligned on what they are ultimately trying to build. Even routine tasks feel different when connected to something meaningful. Vision, in this sense, is not only a strategic instrument. It is a social climate condition.

The contrast is vivid in organizations undergoing change. In one public health agency navigating a difficult restructuring, a director took time each month to revisit the team's founding purpose with staff—not to paper over the difficulty but to help people see it in context. The restructuring was painful; some positions were eliminated. But because people retained a sense of shared direction, the team held together. Collaboration continued. Cynicism, though present, did not calcify. In a comparable agency nearby, the same structural changes were made without that sustained attention to direction. Within a year, turnover had doubled and trust in leadership had collapsed. The external circumstances were nearly identical. The social climate outcomes were not.

In the presence of a shared vision, people:

- share common values,
- listen to each other,
- make decisions in inclusive and respectful ways,
- cooperate,
- share responsibility for making things work,
- have clear and consistent goals, and
- give one another the freedom to do things in our own way.

In its absence, people may work hard yet feel disconnected from outcomes. Short-term pressures dominate, and cynicism grows as effort appears detached from progress.

Strengthening a Shared Vision

Actions that support this dimension include:

- Articulating clear and humane goals that reflect shared values
- Coordinating efforts
- Linking everyday work to longer-term aims

- Revisiting and refining the vision as conditions evolve
- Inviting broad participation in shaping and sustaining it

Participation here does not mean reaching full consensus—that is rarely possible in complex societies. It means creating genuine opportunities for people to shape the goals that will govern their collective life, and taking those contributions seriously when decisions are made.

A flourishing society treats vision as a living process, not a static declaration. A vision that is revisited becomes a site of ongoing collective reflection. One that is only proclaimed becomes wallpaper.

Positive Outlook: Realistic Hope and Collective Efficacy

A positive outlook does not mean ignoring difficulty or denying harm. It is a realistic hope—the belief that problems can be addressed, that effort can make a difference, and that improvement is possible.

The distinction between realistic hope and either naïve optimism or learned helplessness is worth dwelling on. Naïve optimism denies difficulty—it insists things are fine when they are not, dismisses concerns as negativity, and eventually collapses on contact with reality. Learned helplessness accepts difficulty but treats it as permanent—nothing will change, effort is futile, things have always been this way and always will be. Realistic hope occupies a different position entirely. It acknowledges difficulty honestly, names setbacks for what they are, and still maintains that something can be done. It is the stance of people who have looked closely at a problem and, based on evidence and character, chosen to remain engaged.

This distinction matters because the two failure modes—denial and fatalism—call for completely different responses. A community gripped by naïve optimism needs honest conversation about what is actually happening. A community gripped by fatalism needs visible evidence that effort produces results. Confusing the two produces interventions that make things worse: confronting a despairing community with enforced positivity, or introducing critical analysis into a group that needs encouragement, can each deepen the problem it was meant to solve. A flourishing society develops the capacity to distinguish between them.

One of the most effective ways to build realistic hope is to make progress visible. A neighborhood cleanup initiative that posts before-and-after photographs, a school that shares data each term on improved attendance alongside honest acknowledgment of remaining challenges, a workplace team that opens its monthly meeting by naming one thing that worked and one thing that did not—each of these practices trains people to see change as real and possible without demanding that they ignore what is hard. Over time, this kind of practice reshapes a community's interpretive habits. People begin to see difficulty as information rather than a verdict, and effort as an investment rather than futility.

When a positive outlook is present, people:

- maintain high standards,
- have a high level of team spirit,
- resolve conflicts in positive ways,
- celebrate achievements,
- have a can-do attitude, and
- are proud of our group.

When it is absent, pessimism hardens into fatalism. People disengage, lower expectations, and stop investing in collective solutions—even when change is possible.

Strengthening a Positive Outlook

Actions that support this dimension include:

- Naming challenges honestly without catastrophizing
- Highlighting progress and learning alongside problems
- Reinforcing narratives of agency and cooperation
- Celebrating meaningful—even incremental—successes

A flourishing society actively challenges narratives that cast distress as inevitable or improvement as futile. Such narratives are rarely announced openly; they spread through tone, silence, and repeated experience. When problems are raised and nothing changes, when successes go unacknowledged, when humor disappears from shared life, the message accumulates: things cannot be different. Countering this requires not just communication but visible action—demonstrating, repeatedly and concretely, that effort leads somewhere.

How the Three Elements Work Together

These three elements—community, vision, and outlook—are mutually reinforcing.

- A sense of community strengthens commitment to a shared vision.
- A shared vision gives the community direction and coherence.
- A positive outlook energizes both individuals and institutions to persist through difficulty.

When all three are present, social life feels navigable and purposeful. When one or more are missing, strain appears elsewhere in the system. Efforts to strengthen the social climate are most effective when they address all three dimensions together.

Social Climate as a Shared Responsibility

No single institution or leader owns the social climate. Everyday interactions, informal norms, peer behavior, leadership decisions, and institutional design across society shape it. Everyone contributes to creating it—often without realizing it.

In a flourishing society, this shared responsibility is recognized. People understand that how they speak, listen, include, and respond shapes a shared emotional and psychological environment. Leadership, peers, and institutions work together to reinforce a sense of belonging, direction, and hope.

Social Climate and Societal Flourishing

Ultimately, social climate is one of the clearest indicators of societal flourishing. A society may have sophisticated systems and advanced technologies yet remain deeply strained if its social climate is fragmented, directionless, or despairing.

A flourishing society attends to this invisible yet powerful dimension of life together. It measures it, discusses it, and deliberately strengthens it—recognizing that a healthy social climate does not merely reflect well-being but actively produces it.

Think of what it feels like to walk into a room where people are genuinely glad to see each other, where the work feels connected to something worth doing, and where difficulty is met with energy rather than resignation. Now think of its opposite: a room where eyes avoid, where effort feels pointless, where even good news lands flat. The difference between the two rooms is in their social climate. It can be present in a classroom, a workplace, a neighborhood, or a nation. And it is not fixed. A flourishing society bets, with good evidence, that this is one of the most important things it can tend to.

Diagnostic Questions: Social Climate in a Flourishing Society

The following questions help assess whether the social climate supports or undermines well-being, engagement, and collective capacity.

I. Sense of Community

Do people experience belonging, trust, and mutual responsibility?

- Do people feel they belong and are valued as members of the group or society?
- Do people get to know one another?
- Are relationships generally characterized by trust rather than suspicion?
- Do people notice and care when others are absent or struggling?
- Are differences handled with respect and curiosity rather than avoidance or hostility?
- Do people feel safe participating without fear of exclusion or humiliation?

Diagnostic signal: A weak sense of community manifests as isolation, guardedness, and disengagement—even when people are physically together.

II. Shared Vision

Is there a clear and humane sense of direction?

- Do people understand what the group or society is trying to achieve?
- Is there clarity about why these goals matter?
- Can people see how daily efforts contribute to shared aims?
- Are trade-offs openly discussed in light of flourishing values?

- Is the vision revisited and refined as conditions change?

Diagnostic signal: Without shared vision, effort fragments and meaning erodes.

III. Positive Outlook

Do people hold realistic hope and a sense of collective efficacy?

- Do people believe problems can be addressed through collective effort?
- Are setbacks viewed as temporary and manageable rather than permanent or overwhelming?
- Is difficulty discussed honestly, without denial or catastrophizing?
- Are learning and improvement emphasized alongside challenges?
- Do people celebrate individual and collective accomplishments?
- Do people have opportunities for fun?

Diagnostic signal: Loss of positive outlook often precedes withdrawal, cynicism, and burnout.

IV. Everyday Experience of the Social Climate

How does the social climate feel in daily life?

- Is the general tone respectful and constructive?
- Do interactions leave people energized more often than depleted?
- Are appreciation and recognition common?
- Is humor used to build connection rather than demean?
- Do people feel psychologically safe speaking up?

Diagnostic signal: A chronically tense, indifferent, or dismissive tone signals climate strain.

V. Impact on Well-Being and Productivity

What outcomes are associated with the current climate?

- Are stress, burnout, or disengagement widespread?
- Do people sustain energy and motivation over time?
- Is collaboration generally effective?
- Are mistakes addressed without excessive fear?
- Do people remain invested in improvement?

Diagnostic signal: When well-being and productivity decline together, social climate is often a contributing factor.

VI. Responsiveness and Adaptation

Can the social climate be strengthened intentionally?

- Are concerns about social climate noticed and taken seriously?
- Do leaders and peers act to improve conditions when needed?
- Are small improvements tracked and celebrated?
- Can the group learn from experience?

Diagnostic signal: Inability to reflect on or improve climate signals, indicating a declining collective capacity.

VII. Integrative Questions

How well do the three elements reinforce one another?

- Does a sense of community support the shared vision?
- Does the shared vision strengthen optimism and effort?
- Does a positive outlook reinforce belonging and engagement?
- Are all three present to some degree—or is one compensating for the others' absence?

Diagnostic signal: A sustainable social climate requires strengths across all three dimensions.

Using the Diagnostic

These questions are intended to surface patterns, not assign blame. A healthy social climate does not require constant positivity or unanimity. It requires belonging, direction, and hope—supported by norms, peer behavior, and leadership practices.

A flourishing society attends to the social climate because it is one of the most powerful—and most modifiable—determinants of collective well-being and effectiveness.

PART II

INSTITUTIONS AND SYSTEMS – WHERE CULTURE BECOMES CONCRETE

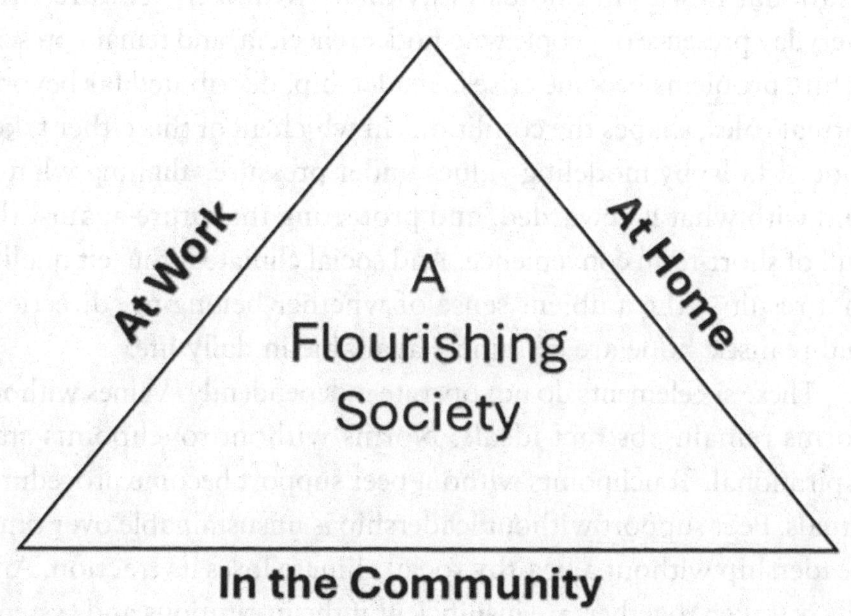

The previous section explored six elements that together constitute the cultural foundations of a flourishing society. Shared flourishing values—commitments to dignity, health, productive work, joy, kindness, learning, and connection—form the bedrock: the deepest layer of agreement about what a good society is actually for. Cultural norms translate those values into lived expectations, providing the shared behavioral framework—clear enough to reduce anxiety, flexible enough to accommodate human diversity—that makes cooperation possible without demanding conformity. Touchpoints are the recurring encounters through which norms are either lived or quietly contradicted: every reward, ritual, conversation, and symbol either reinforces what a society says it values or reveals the gap between declaration and practice. Peer support forms the relational fabric that holds individuals within the culture—the everyday presence of people who notice, check in, and remain present before problems become crises. Leadership, distributed far beyond formal roles, shapes the conditions in which all of this either takes root or fails: by modeling values under pressure, aligning what is said with what is rewarded, and protecting the future against the pull of short-term convenience. And social climate is the felt quality that results—the ambient sense of whether belonging, direction, and realistic hope are genuinely available in daily life.

These six elements do not operate independently. Values without norms remain abstract ideals. Norms without touchpoints stay aspirational. Touchpoints without peer support become procedural rituals. Peer support without leadership is unsustainable over time. Leadership without a healthy social climate loses its traction. And all six, taken together, are insufficient if the institutions and systems that structure daily life are pulling in the opposite direction.

This insight reveals the next level of analysis. Culture does not exist in abstraction. It becomes real—or fails to—through the institutions and systems that shape how people work, learn, care for one another, govern themselves, and make sense of the world.

Social institutions and systems are enduring structures that organize a society's essential functions, distribute roles and resources, transmit values, and coordinate collective life. Systems refer to the dynamic networks of relationships, policies, and feedback loops through which institutions operate and influence one another. Institutions and systems provide stability and continuity across generations while shaping individuals' daily experiences, expectations, and opportunities.

Together, institutions and systems form the scaffolding of social life.

Key Examples of Social Institutions

- **Family systems** – Structures that organize caregiving, socialization, emotional development, and intergenerational support.
- **Educational systems** – Schools, universities, and training institutions that cultivate knowledge, skills, and civic capacity.
- **Economic and financial systems** – Markets, firms, labor systems, banking, and capital allocation mechanisms that organize production and distribution.
- **Government and legal systems** – Political institutions, regulatory frameworks, courts, and democratic processes that establish rules and protect rights.
- **Health care systems** – Hospitals, clinics, insurers, and public health agencies that promote physical and mental well-being.
- **Religious and spiritual institutions** – Communities and traditions that transmit meaning, moral guidance, and shared identity.

- **Media and communication systems** – Journalism, digital platforms, and cultural industries that shape information flow and public discourse.
- **Technology systems** – Infrastructure and innovation networks that mediate how people connect, work, and access information.

Why This Matters for Flourishing

In a flourishing society, institutions align with shared values that uphold dignity, learning, health, productive contribution, joy, and connection. When institutions become misaligned with human needs—through rigidity, inequity, fragmentation, or short-term orientation—they can unintentionally create strain, isolation, or instability.

Because institutions are designed and maintained by people, they are not fixed. They can evolve. And when they evolve in ways that support human capacity rather than undermine it, they become powerful engines of flourishing.

Social institutions and systems do more than deliver services. They organize experience, allocate resources and authority, define roles and expectations, and establish what is considered legitimate, normal, or possible. When institutions align with human needs, they stabilize and reinforce societal flourishing. When they are misaligned, they can quietly normalize strain, alienation, and moral compromise—even while appearing efficient or successful.

A flourishing society, therefore, pays close attention to how its institutions function—not only what they accomplish but also how they shape the lives of the people within them.

These are not separate from culture. They are culture operationalized. Institutions translate values into incentives. They convert norms into policies. They embody leadership through structure. They shape the social climate at scale.

If the six cultural elements are the DNA of a society, institutions are the living body through which that DNA is expressed.

In this section, we examine how key systems either support or undermine flourishing—and how they can be redesigned to foster supportive cultural environments.

A Note on Structure

Each chapter in this book examines a different institution or domain of social life—families, schools, workplaces, communities, and others—through a consistent lens. That lens is organized around four questions: How can this institution embody the core flourishing values of productive work, health, joy, kindness, learning, and connection? What conditions does the broader society need to provide for this institution to thrive? How might flourishing within it be meaningfully assessed? And how would a flourishing societal culture help this institution achieve its own deepest goals?

This repeated structure is intentional. Flourishing is not a collection of unrelated goods. It is a coherent way of living and organizing life together. By applying the same framework across different contexts, this book aims to show that these values are not abstract ideals suited only to certain settings. They are portable. They scale. They are as relevant in a classroom as in a boardroom, as germane at a family dinner table as in a hospital ward.

Readers familiar with one chapter will find the framework immediately recognizable in the next. That familiarity is an invitation—to notice how the same values manifest differently depending on context, and to consider how institutions that seem quite unlike one another are, at their best, working toward the same ends.

A flourishing society is not built in one place. It is built everywhere—in the small repeated choices of institutions that share a common commitment to human dignity, growth, and connection.

Chapter 8

The Role of Technology and Innovation in a Flourishing Society

TECHNOLOGY AND INNOVATION are not neutral forces. They are cultural expressions. Every tool, system, and platform embodies assumptions about what matters, whose needs count, which risks are acceptable, and what kind of future is desirable. In this sense, technology does not simply change society; it reveals society.

In a flourishing society, technology and innovation are guided by values that support flourishing. They are developed and deployed in ways that reflect care for human dignity, well-being, community, and the natural world. They are evaluated not solely for efficiency, profit, or novelty but for their long-term impact on human and environmental health.

The question is not whether a society innovates. It is whether innovation is aligned with flourishing—and whether the social conditions exist to keep asking that question honestly.

Technology as a Reflection of Flourishing Values

Every innovation answers an implicit question: What problem are we trying to solve, and for whom? A flourishing society begins with that question—and insists on returning to it as circumstances change.

Consider the domain of work. If a society values meaningful contributions, technology should support them rather than indiscriminately displace them. Automation and artificial intelligence hold genuine promise: they can reduce drudgery, improve workplace safety, and expand creative capacity. But the record is uneven. The introduction of warehouse management algorithms at companies like Amazon has improved throughput while generating documented harms—injury rates substantially higher than industry averages, surveillance systems that track workers to the second, and an attrition model that treats human turnover as a design feature rather than a warning sign. A flourishing society would recognize these outcomes not as inevitable consequences of progress but as design choices, and would insist on different ones.

Consider health. Digital tools have expanded access to care in important ways—telehealth consultations now reach patients in rural and underserved areas who previously had little access to specialists. During the COVID-19 pandemic, telehealth visits increased dramatically, and patient satisfaction remained high. But the same technologies can fragment care when poorly implemented: automated triage systems that misclassify symptoms, electronic health records that consume clinician time without improving outcomes, and diagnostic algorithms trained on unrepresentative data that perform worse for patients of color. Innovation in supporting health, to be genuinely beneficial, must be evaluated not only on efficiency but also on affordability and accuracy, and on whether it preserves the human relationships that make medicine work.

Consider connection. Social media platforms were designed to increase engagement—and they succeeded. But the business model that drives engagement has produced consequences their architects did not publicly anticipate and were slow to address. Internal research at Meta, disclosed through whistleblower Frances Haugen in 2021, showed that the company's own data linked Instagram use to depression and body image harm in adolescent girls. Algorithms optimized for attention reliably amplify outrage over information. A flourishing society treats these findings not as public-relations problems but as design failures that demand correction.

These examples share a common lesson: the values embedded in technology are not fixed at the time of invention. They are negotiated through policy, culture, regulation, and the persistent pressure of communities that insist on better. A flourishing society maintains that pressure.

How a Flourishing Society Supports Responsible Innovation

A flourishing society does not merely constrain technology—it creates the conditions in which the best kind of innovation becomes possible. This is a point worth dwelling on, because it reframes the relationship between social values and technological progress.

When a culture genuinely values learning, curiosity, and long-term well-being, individuals and institutions are more likely to invest in research that addresses meaningful problems rather than merely profitable ones. Open science norms, which depend on a culture of trust and shared purpose, accelerate discovery by enabling researchers to build on one another's work rather than guard it. The collaborative character of the internet's foundational protocols, developed in a culture of academic openness, produced more durable and interoperable infrastructure than a purely proprietary approach would have.

Supportive social climates also reduce the fear of failure that routinely stifles creativity. In societies where failure is treated as a learning experience rather than a disgrace, experimentation is more common, more honest, and more productive. Research on innovation ecosystems consistently finds that psychological safety—the confidence that one can raise concerns, propose unconventional ideas, or acknowledge mistakes without penalty—is among the strongest predictors of creative output at both the team and organizational level. A flourishing society cultivates this climate not only in laboratories and startups but in schools, institutions, and communities.

Trust matters especially. When citizens trust public institutions and when institutions trust communities, the conditions for responsible innovation improve substantially. Clinical trial recruitment is easier in high-trust environments. Regulatory oversight is more effective when it is seen as collaborative rather than adversarial. Communities are more willing to host new infrastructure—such as renewable energy installations, research facilities, and public health programs—when they believe their interests will be genuinely considered. The erosion of institutional trust that characterizes many contemporary societies is not simply a political problem; it is an innovation problem.

Finally, a flourishing society expands the range of people who participate in innovation. Diversity in research and development—across gender, race, class, geography, and discipline—consistently produces more robust and broadly applicable solutions. Homogeneous teams are more likely to build tools that work well for people like themselves and miss the needs of everyone else. When algorithmic hiring tools, trained primarily on historical data reflecting past biases, reproduce those biases in their recommendations, it is partly a technical failure and partly a failure of inclusion in who built the system and whose interests shaped its design criteria.

In short, innovation driven by competition and short-term profit alone tends to optimize for narrow outcomes. Innovation embedded in a flourishing society—one characterized by trust, shared purpose, psychological safety, and broad participation—is more likely to be responsible, durable, and genuinely beneficial.

Innovation and Environmental Stewardship

No society can claim to flourish while undermining the ecological systems that sustain life. This is not an abstract principle—it is an increasingly urgent practical constraint. And technology sits at the center of the tension.

The energy demands of digital infrastructure are substantial and growing. Training a single large AI language model can emit carbon emissions comparable to those of several automobiles over its lifetime. Global data centers collectively consume roughly one to two percent of worldwide electricity—a figure expected to rise as AI adoption accelerates. At its peak, cryptocurrency mining rivaled the annual electricity usage of entire countries. These are not arguments against computation; they are arguments for designing it with environmental costs as first-order considerations rather than afterthoughts.

At the same time, technology offers some of the most powerful tools available for environmental restoration. Smart grid systems improve the efficiency of renewable energy distribution. Satellite and sensor networks enable real-time monitoring of deforestation, ocean health, and atmospheric conditions. Precision agriculture reduces water and pesticide use while maintaining yields. The question a flourishing society asks is not whether to innovate but whether environmental costs are honestly accounted for—in design decisions, pricing models, regulation, and public discourse—rather than externalized onto vulnerable communities and future generations.

Environmental sustainability is not an optional add-on. It is a foundational requirement for long-term flourishing. A society that treats it otherwise is borrowing capacity from the future and calling it progress.

Technology, Human Needs, and the Limits of Efficiency

Innovation in a flourishing society remains grounded in fundamental human needs: belonging, meaning, agency, safety, and growth. Efficiency is a legitimate and important goal—but in a flourishing society, it is subordinate to these deeper purposes, not their replacement.

The efficiency trap is real and well-documented. Digital systems that eliminate human contact in the name of speed often exact a high hidden cost. Automated customer service systems reduce labor expenses while generating documented frustration and, for vulnerable users, genuine distress. Algorithmic decision-making in high-stakes domains—criminal sentencing, credit scoring, child welfare screening—can improve consistency while embedding and amplifying existing biases, replacing moral judgment with a kind of laundered prejudice that is harder to contest precisely because it appears objective.

Data-informed decision-making, similarly, should enhance human judgment rather than substitute for it. When a parole algorithm assigns a risk score to a defendant, the question is not only whether the score is statistically valid on average but whether it is just in the particular case before a particular judge—and whether the people most affected by such systems have any meaningful voice in how they are designed.

Concern for human needs also requires inclusive design from the start. Innovation must account for differences in ability, age, language, income, and cultural context. Accessibility is not charity; it is recognition of shared dignity—and it tends to produce better products for everyone. The curb-cut effect, named for sidewalk ramps designed for wheelchair users that also benefit cyclists, parents with strollers, and delivery workers, illustrates a broader principle: designing for those at the margins often improves the experience at the center.

A flourishing society resists the temptation to treat users as data points or markets. It remembers that every innovation ultimately shapes lived experience—and insists that shaping it well is worth the effort.

Collective Learning and the Governance of Change

A defining characteristic of a flourishing society is its ability to learn collectively and adapt responsibly to new realities. Technology accelerates change; flourishing requires that reflection keep pace.

This is harder than it sounds. Regulatory frameworks have consistently lagged behind technological development—not because policymakers are indifferent but because the pace of change outstrips the institutional capacity to understand and respond to it. Social media platforms operated with minimal meaningful oversight for more than a decade before legislative attention caught up, by which point their architectures were entrenched, and their effects on democratic discourse were already substantial. Generative AI is following a similar trajectory: capabilities are advancing rapidly, applications are proliferating, and governance frameworks are only beginning to take shape.

A flourishing society does not accept this lag as inevitable. It invests in institutions capable of learning at the speed of change—regulatory bodies with genuine technical expertise, public deliberation processes that include affected communities, and norms of transparency that enable harm to be identified before it becomes irreversible. It treats ethical dialogue not as a brake on innovation but as a condition of legitimate innovation. And it maintains the institutional humility to revise, pause, or withdraw technologies whose harms outweigh their benefits—even when those technologies are profitable.

Openness to diverse perspectives is not merely procedural. The communities most affected by technological systems are often those least consulted in their design. Facial recognition technology, deployed in policing and security contexts, was shown by researchers Joy Buolamwini and Timnit Gebru to have significantly higher error rates for darker-skinned women than for lighter-skinned men. This failure predictably fell hardest on the people with the least power to contest it. A flourishing society makes the inclusion of affected voices in innovation processes a structural requirement, not an optional gesture.

Guarding Against Fragmentation

Technology has extraordinary power to connect—and to divide. This is not a paradox; it is a design consequence. Platforms built to maximize engagement have learned that outrage, fear, and tribal identity are among the most reliable drivers of attention. The result is a media environment in which algorithms systematically amplify conflict and erode the shared epistemic ground on which democratic deliberation depends.

The evidence here is sobering. Studies of online political discourse have found that exposure to opposing views on algorithmically curated platforms often increases polarization rather than reducing it, because the most extreme and emotionally charged content travels furthest. Misinformation spreads faster than corrections. Communities fracture along lines that platforms did not create but reliably exploit.

A flourishing society pays attention to how technologies influence the social climate—not to enforce consensus but to recognize that some minimum of shared reality and mutual respect is a precondition for collective problem-solving. This means holding platforms accountable for their algorithmic choices, investing in digital and media literacy, supporting local journalism and civic information ecosystems, and being willing to regulate as a last resort when market incentives reliably produce public harm.

Innovation as Stewardship

Perhaps the most important reframing this chapter proposes is this: innovation in a flourishing society is not merely creative disruption. It is stewardship.

The language of disruption—celebrated in business culture for decades—frames change as inherently valuable, speed as inherently virtuous, and existing arrangements as inherently obstacles. Stewardship asks different questions: What long-term effects will this have? Who benefits, and who bears the cost? Does this strengthen or weaken our collective capacity? Will it make it easier or harder for future generations to live well?

These are not anti-innovation questions. They are the questions that distinguish innovation that genuinely serves human flourishing from innovation that merely accelerates change for those positioned to profit from it. When applied seriously, they tend to produce technology that is more durable, more equitable, and more worthy of public trust—precisely because broader purposes than the market alone have shaped it.

When innovation is guided by stewardship, it becomes a force for resilience and renewal rather than for instability and extraction. That is the ambition a flourishing society holds for its most creative energies.

Technology Within a Broader Cultural System

Technology does not operate independently of culture. It interacts with norms, leadership, peer relationships, institutions, and social climate in ways that are reciprocal and often unpredictable. A new platform does not simply reflect existing social dynamics; it amplifies some and suppresses others, reshapes incentives, and creates new possibilities for both connection and harm.

A flourishing society, therefore, integrates technology into its broader efforts to shape a healthy culture. It examines how digital tools influence peer relationships and social comparison. It considers how automation affects work, family time, and community stability. It asks how algorithmic systems shape the information environments in which political and moral judgments are made. And it attends to the narratives of progress that frame public expectations—recognizing that the story a society tells about technology shapes what it is willing to demand of it.

Innovation is one lever among many—powerful, consequential, and accountable to broader human purposes. Treating it as anything less is not realistic. It is abdication.

A Future Worth Building

Technology and innovation hold extraordinary potential. They can reduce suffering, expand opportunity, deepen knowledge, restore environmental balance, and connect human beings across distances that once made solidarity impossible. They can also intensify inequity, accelerate stress, undermine democratic institutions, and fragment the communities they claim to serve.

The difference lies not in the tools themselves but in the values that guide them—and in whether culture and institutions enforce those values, and in the persistent insistence of citizens who refuse to accept that harm is inevitable.

A flourishing society approaches this challenge with both ambition and humility. It neither romanticizes the past nor fears the future. It asks, continuously and collectively, whether the technologies it is building reflect the kind of society it is trying to become. And it maintains the institutional capacity, the civic culture, and the moral seriousness to answer that question honestly—and to act on the answer.

When guided by shared values, supported by humane institutions, and held accountable by an engaged public, technology becomes not a threat to flourishing but one of its most powerful allies.

Diagnostic Questions: Technology and Innovation in a Flourishing Society

The preceding analysis points toward a practical question: how do we evaluate specific technologies and innovations against these standards? The following diagnostic is designed for that purpose. It can be used by design teams, policy bodies, organizational leaders, or community groups assessing whether a particular technology—or a portfolio of innovations—supports dignity, sustainability, and collective well-being. Look for patterns and systemic effects, not isolated features.

I. Alignment with Shared Values

1. Purpose and Human Benefit

- What human need does this innovation aim to address?
- Does it enhance dignity, health, learning, connection, or meaningful contribution?
- Who benefits most—and who might be left out?

***Warning sign:** Innovation is driven primarily by novelty, speed, or profit without a clear human-centered purpose.*

2. Productive Work and Meaning

- Does this technology reduce unnecessary drudgery while preserving meaningful contribution?
- Are displaced roles addressed with dignity and transition support?
- Does it expand human creativity and agency rather than replace them indiscriminately?

***Warning sign:** Efficiency gains erode identity and agency without mitigation.*

II. Impact on Well-Being and Social Climate

3. Attention and Psychological Well-Being

- Does this technology support healthy use patterns?
- Are design features mindful of cognitive load, addiction risk, or anxiety?

- Does it protect space for rest, reflection, and presence?

Warning sign: *Business models depend on capturing and monetizing attention at the expense of well-being.*

4. Connection and Community

- Does this innovation strengthen meaningful relationships?
- Does it promote respectful dialogue and reduce polarization?
- Are safeguards in place to prevent harassment or dehumanization?

Warning sign: *Increased connectivity is accompanied by rising fragmentation or hostility.*

5. Positive Outlook and Collective Agency

- Does the technology help people solve problems collaboratively?
- Does it increase transparency and shared understanding?
- Does it support realistic hope rather than amplify fear?

Warning sign: *Platforms or systems consistently intensify outrage, helplessness, or fatalism.*

III. Environmental Stewardship and Sustainability

6. Environmental Impact

- What are the ecological costs of production, operation, and disposal?
- Does this innovation reduce environmental harm—or shift it elsewhere?
- Are renewable and circular models prioritized?

Warning sign: *Environmental consequences are externalized or ignored.*

7. Intergenerational Responsibility

- How might this innovation affect future generations?
- Are long-term risks evaluated alongside short-term benefits?
- Is sustainability integrated into design decisions?

Warning sign: *Decisions prioritize immediate gains over long-term viability.*

IV. Equity and Inclusion

8. Accessibility and Fairness

- Is the technology accessible across socioeconomic, linguistic, and ability differences?
- Does it reduce barriers—or create new ones?
- Are marginalized groups considered during design and testing?

Warning sign: *Innovation widens disparities in access or opportunity.*

9. Data Ethics and Privacy

- Are data collected transparently and responsibly?
- Do users understand how their information is used?
- Are safeguards in place to prevent misuse or exploitation?

Warning sign: *Data extraction outpaces ethical oversight.*

V. Institutional and System Alignment

10. Policy and Governance

- Are appropriate regulations and oversight in place?
- Is governance adaptive and informed by technical expertise and public input?

- Are public voices—especially those of affected communities—included in shaping technological integration?

Warning sign: *Innovation outpaces governance, and affected communities have no meaningful recourse.*

11. Organizational Culture and Accountability

- Do internal practices—rewards, goals, and communication—support responsible innovation?
- Are employees and researchers encouraged to raise ethical concerns without penalty?
- Is there an independent mechanism for surfacing harms that internal culture might suppress?

Warning sign: *Ethical concerns are dismissed in favor of speed or competition, and dissent is penalized.*

VI. Learning and Adaptive Capacity

12. Openness to Feedback

- Are unintended consequences monitored and addressed?
- Is there a willingness to revise, pause, or withdraw harmful innovations?
- Are evaluation processes transparent and independent?

Warning sign: *Defensiveness replaces reflection; harms are minimized or attributed to user error.*

13. Capacity for Iterative Improvement

- Is innovation treated as an ongoing learning process rather than a completed product?

- Are ethical and social impacts regularly reviewed, including by affected communities?
- Does adaptation occur before crisis forces it?

Core signal of flourishing capacity: *The system can learn and course-correct without harming those within it.*

Integrative Reflection Questions

- Does this innovation make it easier or harder for people to live healthy, connected, and meaningful lives?
- Does it strengthen or weaken the social climate—community, shared vision, and collective agency?
- Does it reduce or increase the structural effort required to flourish?
- Would we be comfortable if this system shaped the lives of our children and grandchildren?
- Does it reflect the kind of society we are trying to become—or the kind we are trying to leave behind?

Using the Diagnostic

This diagnostic is not anti-technology. It is pro-alignment. A flourishing society does not reject innovation—it guides it. These questions are most useful when applied early, when design choices are still open, and when the teams using them include people who represent the full range of those the innovation will affect. When technology reflects shared values, respects human limits, protects the environment, and strengthens collective capacity, it becomes a powerful ally in building a healthier, more humane, and more sustainable future.

Chapter 9

The Role of Business and Finance in a Flourishing Society

FINANCE IS OFTEN treated as a neutral mechanism—an arena of numbers, markets, and instruments removed from moral or social concerns. In reality, finance is among the most powerful cultural forces in any society. It shapes what is built, sustained, rewarded, and neglected. It influences work, health, environmental stability, and intergenerational security. It determines whether risk is shared or shifted and whether opportunity is expanded or restricted.

In a flourishing society, business finance reflects shared values rather than undermining them. It serves as a tool for stewardship, stability, and long-term flourishing rather than short-term extraction.

The question is not whether a society uses finance. It is how finance is guided—and for what ends.

Finance as a Reflection of Values

Financial systems reveal priorities with remarkable clarity. Investment flows show what is considered promising. Insurance pricing reveals what risks are acknowledged and shared. Retirement planning reflects assumptions about aging and dignity. Corporate finance structures signal whether long-term resilience or short-term gain is preferred.

If a society values productive work, finance should support enterprises that make meaningful contributions rather than speculative bubbles that are detached from real value.

If a society values health, financial systems invest in preventive care, mental health integration, and stable working conditions—not just in crisis response.

Finance, in this sense, is a moral language expressed in numbers—and a practical architecture that can either support or obstruct flourishing.

Finance and a Flourishing Economy

A flourishing economy supports broad human capability over time—not merely GDP growth or aggregate wealth. It provides stable livelihoods, enables mobility and opportunity, sustains environmental conditions for future generations, and distributes both risk and reward in ways that reinforce rather than fracture social trust. Finance is the architecture that either builds or undermines such an economy.

A flourishing society strengthens the economy and businesses' performance by fostering cultural conditions that support productivity, innovation, and trust. When societies emphasize productive work, health, joy, kindness, learning, and connection, employees are more engaged, relationships within organizations are more cooperative, and workplaces are better able to attract and retain talent. Healthy and well-supported individuals are more capable of sustained effort, creativity, and problem-solving. At the same time, cultures characterized by trust and shared purpose reduce conflict and transaction costs, making collaboration easier both within and between organizations. Research on organizational culture by scholars such as Daniel Coyle has shown that environments that foster belonging, psychological safety, and shared goals tend to produce stronger performance and innovation. In this way, a flourishing society not only improves the quality of life but also creates the human and cultural foundations that allow businesses and economies to grow in healthy, sustainable ways.

When financial systems are aligned with these conditions—supporting stable employment, fair credit, long-term investment, and shared risk—they amplify flourishing. When they are misaligned—concentrating gains, externalizing costs, or amplifying insecurity—they erode the very foundations of economic vitality.

Income Disparities, Financial Stress, and the Foundations of Flourishing

A flourishing society cannot be built on chronic financial insecurity.

Income disparities matter not only for material differences but also for what those differences signal and produce within a culture. When large segments of the population struggle to meet basic needs—housing, food, health care, education—their cognitive and emotional resources are understandably consumed by short-term survival. Financial stress narrows attention, heightens anxiety, and reduces the bandwidth available for long-term planning, civic participation, learning, and relationship-building. A culture of persistent economic strain becomes one of guardedness rather than generosity.

At the same time, extreme wealth disparities can reshape social norms and expectations. They may weaken shared identity, reduce trust across groups, and foster perceptions of unfairness or exclusion. When rewards seem disconnected from contribution—or upward mobility feels inaccessible—motivation shifts from shared advancement to defensive comparison. This erodes peer support, undermines social cohesion, and destabilizes the broader cultural web that supports flourishing.

Importantly, flourishing does not require uniform outcomes. Income and achievement diversity is inevitable in any dynamic society. What matters is whether economic systems provide:

- **A secure foundation** – so basic needs are reliably met.
- **Fair opportunity pathways** – so effort and talent can realistically lead to growth.
- **Reasonable proportionality** – so disparities do not fracture social trust.
- **Long-term orientation** – so capital strengthens human development rather than extracting short-term gain.

Finance plays a central role in shaping these conditions. Capital allocation decisions, compensation structures, tax policies, access to credit, and investment priorities all determine whether economic life expands or constrains human capacity.

In a flourishing society, financial systems reduce chronic stress rather than amplify it. They enable stability, mobility, and contribution. They help people look beyond survival toward purpose, creativity, connection, and shared progress.

When financial stress becomes widespread and disparities destabilizing, flourishing becomes fragile. When economic foundations are secure and broadly accessible, flourishing becomes possible—and sustainable.

Investment: Allocating the Future

Investment is one of the most powerful levers shaping society's direction. Capital allocation determines which industries grow, which innovations flourish, which jobs are created, and which communities thrive.

In a flourishing economy, investment decisions explicitly consider long-term environmental impact, human well-being and dignity, workforce stability and capability, and community resilience.

This does not require sacrificing profitability. It requires broadening the definition of "value" to include sustainability, risk mitigation, and social trust. Investments that generate short-term returns while eroding environmental or social stability create hidden liabilities that ultimately undermine both markets and well-being.

Insurance: Sharing Risk and Promoting Security

Insurance embodies a profound social principle: risk is shared so that individuals and families are not devastated by unpredictable events. In a flourishing society, insurance systems reflect solidarity rather than exclusion.

Health insurance supports prevention and integrates mental health care. Property insurance incentivizes climate-resilient construction. Disability insurance protects dignity during periods of vulnerability. Social insurance programs (such as unemployment and retirement systems) stabilize families and communities during economic shifts.

When insurance becomes inaccessible, predatory, or narrowly risk-selective, it deepens insecurity. A flourishing society recognizes that widespread insecurity erodes well-being, trust, and civic life. At its best, insurance reinforces the value of people's non-disposability when circumstances change.

Retirement Planning: Dignity Across the Lifespan

How a society organizes retirement reveals its view of aging, contribution, and intergenerational responsibility.

In a flourishing society, retirement planning supports:

- long-term financial stability,
- protection against poverty in later life,
- opportunities for continued meaning and contribution, and
- flexibility in transitioning among work, caregiving, and rest.

Retirement systems that rely solely on individual financial literacy—without adequate institutional support—exacerbate anxiety and inequity. By contrast, systems that combine personal responsibility with collective safeguards foster security and psychological stability.

A society that treats later life as disposable undermines its own continuity. A society that supports dignified aging strengthens its moral coherence and intergenerational trust.

Corporate Finance and Organizational Responsibility

Within enterprises, financial decision-making directly shapes culture. Compensation systems, investment in learning and development, budgeting priorities, pricing models, and performance metrics all influence norms, social climate, and everyday well-being.

Financial models that…

- reward long-term performance over quarterly spikes,
- invest in workforce health, learning, and retention
- incorporate environmental costs into planning

…tend to support resilience and sustained contribution.

When corporate finance prioritizes short-term shareholder returns above all else, organizations may face rising burnout, moral injury, eroding trust, and a weakened social climate—even if profits appear strong in the near term.

A flourishing society fosters financial frameworks that recognize employees, communities, and ecosystems as stakeholders—not merely as inputs.

Access, Inclusion, and Financial Capability

Financial systems also shape inclusion. Access to banking, credit, fair lending, and clear financial guidance determines whether individuals and families can build stability.

In a flourishing society:

- financial services are accessible and transparent,
- predatory practices are regulated and constrained
- people are supported in understanding financial decisions.

Financial capability is not only a personal skill but also a public good. Money-related anxiety is among the most persistent stressors in modern life. Reducing unnecessary complexity, volatility, and exploitation directly supports flourishing by making daily life more predictable, manageable, and planful.

Finance and Environmental Sustainability

The financial system has a substantial influence on environmental outcomes. Investment in fossil fuels, deforestation, and extractive industries accelerates climate risk, while investment in renewable energy, regenerative agriculture, and sustainable infrastructure mitigates it.

In a flourishing society, financial institutions:

- incorporate climate risk into decision-making,

- shift capital toward sustainable systems, and
- treat environmental degradation as both a financial risk and a moral failure.

Sustainability is not peripheral to finance—it is central to long-term stability, health, and prosperity.

Balancing Risk, Reward, and Responsibility

Markets entail risk and reward. A flourishing society does not eliminate risk; it distributes risk responsibly and transparently.

This requires:

- ethical standards in advising and product design,
- regulation that protects against systemic collapse,
- oversight to prevent fraud and exploitation, and
- alignment between private incentives and public well-being.

Financial crises often expose cultural distortions—speculation detached from value, misaligned incentives, opacity, and short-termism. A flourishing society treats these not only as technical problems but as cultural problems, requiring reforms in norms, leadership expectations, and accountability.

Finance as Stewardship

At its best, business finance is a form of stewardship—managing resources today to support stability and opportunity tomorrow. It supports families, funds innovation, insures against hardship, and enables public and private infrastructure.

At its worst, finance becomes extractive—concentrating wealth, externalizing harm, and amplifying insecurity.

The difference lies in alignment with shared values and institutional responsibility.

In a flourishing society, finance reflects a commitment to human dignity, environmental sustainability, intergenerational security, and collective resilience. It supports productive work without exploiting it. It addresses vulnerability without stigmatizing it. It plans for retirement without creating chronic anxiety. It invests in innovation without ignoring social and ecological costs.

Finance is not separate from culture—it is one of its most powerful expressions. When aligned with flourishing, it becomes a stabilizing foundation for healthier, more secure, and more hopeful lives.

Diagnostic Questions: Finance and Financial Institutions in a Flourishing Society

Finance shapes what grows, what survives, and who feels secure. The following questions help assess whether financial systems support dignity, sustainability, and collective well-being—or quietly undermine them. Look for systemic patterns, not isolated transactions.

I. Alignment with Shared Values

1. Purpose and Stewardship

- Does the institution articulate a purpose beyond short-term profit?
- Are long-term human and environmental outcomes considered in decision-making?
- Is finance viewed as stewardship of resources across generations?

Warning sign: Profit is pursued without regard for downstream consequences.

2. Productive Work

- Do investments support enterprises that make a meaningful contribution?
- Are workforce well-being and stability considered in capital allocation?
- Are restructuring decisions weighed against human and community impact?

Warning sign: Efficiency gains routinely erode dignity without mitigation.

3. Well-Being and Security

- Do financial practices reduce or increase stress for individuals and families?
- Are products transparent and easy to understand?
- Are predatory or exploitative practices actively avoided?

Warning sign: Complexity and opacity heighten anxiety and mistrust.

II. Investment Practices

4. Long-Term Orientation

- Are investments evaluated for long-term resilience?
- Are short-term returns balanced against durability and sustainability?
- Are systemic risks (climate, inequality, instability) incorporated into the analysis?

Warning sign: Quarterly performance overrides long-term stability.

5. Environmental Stewardship

- Are environmental risks integrated into portfolio decisions?
- Is capital allocated to sustainable and regenerative industries?
- Are environmental harms treated as financial risks, rather than externalities?

Warning sign: Ecological degradation is tolerated if profitable.

6. Social Impact

- Do investment strategies consider effects on communities?
- Are labor practices, human rights, and equity assessed?
- Is impact measured alongside financial returns?

Warning sign: Social harm is treated as someone else's problem.

III. Insurance and Risk Sharing

7. Risk Distribution

- Does insurance spread risk fairly?
- Are vulnerable populations protected?
- Are products structured to stabilize rather than destabilize households and families?

Warning sign: Risk is shifted onto those least able to bear it.

8. Incentives for Prevention

- Do insurance models incentivize health, safety, and resilience?
- Are prevention and early intervention supported?
- Does coverage encourage long-term protective behavior?

Warning sign: Crisis response is prioritized over prevention.

IV. Retirement and Long-Term Security

9. Dignity Across the Lifespan

- Do retirement systems offer realistic paths to long-term security?
- Are individuals provided with accessible and trustworthy guidance?
- Are demographic and intergenerational realities considered?

Warning sign: Late-life insecurity is widespread and normalized.

V. Organizational Culture Within Financial Institutions

10. Leadership Integrity

- Do leaders model ethical decision-making?
- Are conflicts of interest disclosed and managed?
- Is honesty prioritized, especially during downturns?

Warning sign: Cultural pressure discourages raising ethical concerns.

11. Incentive Structures

- Do compensation models promote long-term value creation?
- Are incentives aligned with risk management and sustainability?
- Do metrics reinforce responsible conduct?

Warning sign: Short-term gains are rewarded despite the presence of systemic risk.

12. Learning and Accountability

- Are failures examined transparently?

- Is there capacity for institutional learning?
- Are corrective measures implemented before crises escalate?

Warning sign: Defensive culture resists reflection.

VI. Inclusion and Access

13. Financial Access

- Are services accessible across income levels and demographics?
- Are barriers to credit or banking reduced?
- Is financial capability treated as a public good?

Warning sign: Entire populations are excluded from participation.

14. Equity and Fairness

- Are lending and underwriting practices free of bias?
- Is pricing transparent and justifiable?
- Are communities protected from exploitation?

Warning sign: Inequities persist unexamined and uncorrected.

VII. Impact on Social Climate

15. Stability and Trust

- Do financial systems promote confidence and predictability?
- Is public trust in financial institutions strong?
- Are disruptions managed in ways that preserve dignity and cohesion?

Warning sign: Repeated instability erodes trust and increases anxiety.

16. Contribution to Collective Capacity

- Does finance enable investment in education, health, infrastructure, and innovation?
- Are resources mobilized during collective challenges?
- Does financial decision-making strengthen or weaken shared purpose?

Warning sign: Finance amplifies fragmentation or distrust.

VIII. Integrative Reflection Questions

- Does this financial system make it easier or harder for people to live stable, healthy lives?
- Does it encourage stewardship rather than extraction?
- Would we be comfortable if these practices shaped our children's and grandchildren's lives?
- Does finance serve society—or has society been reorganized to serve finance?

Using the Diagnostic

This diagnosis is not anti-market. Markets can be powerful tools for coordination and innovation. The issue is alignment.

A flourishing society expects finance to:

- support productive work,
- protect against vulnerability,
- steward environmental resources,
- reduce unnecessary insecurity, and
- reinforce long-term stability.

When finance fulfills these roles, it becomes a stabilizing foundation for healthier, happier, and more resilient lives.

Chapter 10

The Role of Families in a Flourishing Society

FAMILIES ARE THE first and most influential cultural environments most people encounter. Long before individuals enter schools, workplaces, or civic institutions, they absorb patterns of communication, expectations for effort, norms for emotional expression, and models for handling conflict and care. In this sense, families are not merely private arrangements; they are foundational social institutions. They shape the emotional, cognitive, and moral architecture on which the rest of society is built.

A flourishing society depends on flourishing family cultures. And flourishing family cultures do not emerge by accident. They are cultivated through shared values, consistent norms, intentional leadership, supportive peer relationships, and the reinforcement of daily practices.

Public policies, workplace practices, educational systems, and community norms shape whether families can serve as sources of stability and care, or are left to absorb pressures generated elsewhere in society.

In a flourishing society, families are recognized as essential contributors to collective well-being rather than isolated units expected to cope on their own. Family life is understood to require supportive conditions rather than perfection.

Healthy families in a flourishing society tend to:

- provide emotional safety and reliable care,
- foster connection, trust, and mutual responsibility,
- model communication, conflict repair, and kindness,
- support learning, self-expression, and the development of autonomy, and
- adapt roles as circumstances and life stages change.

Families also serve as a primary context for peer support, where care flows in multiple directions—between partners, across generations, and among siblings or chosen family members. In this way, families mirror—at a smaller scale—the broader capacities a flourishing society seeks to cultivate.

When families are unsupported, overburdened, or isolated, strain often manifests as individual distress, relationship breakdown, or intergenerational stress. A flourishing society does not interpret these outcomes as private failures. Instead, it examines whether families have access to:

- economic security,
- time and flexibility,
- health and mental health support,
- parenting and caregiving resources, and
- social networks that reduce isolation.

This chapter examines how families can embody the core flourishing values of productive work, health, joy, kindness, learning, and connection; how broader society can support thriving family cultures; and how family flourishing can be meaningfully assessed.

I. Flourishing Values Within Family Culture

A family's culture is not defined by perfection or constant harmony. It is defined by patterns—what is encouraged, modeled, rewarded, and repaired when strained.

1. Productive Work

In flourishing families, work is framed not merely as an obligation but as a contribution. Children observe adults engaged in purposeful effort. Responsibilities—age-appropriate chores, shared tasks, and participation in decision-making—are treated as meaningful contributions to the household's collective good.

Productive work in family culture includes:

- Shared responsibility for household functioning
- Recognition of effort, not only outcomes
- Conversations about purpose and contribution
- Modeling perseverance through setbacks

When work is presented as a way to participate in something larger than oneself, it fosters agency, competence, and dignity.

2. Health

Healthy family cultures support physical, emotional, and relational well-being. Flourishing families prioritize:

- adequate sleep, nutrition, and physical activity,
- open discussion of emotions,
- constructive conflict resolution, and
- seeking support when needed.

Rather than stigmatizing struggle, thriving families normalize vulnerability and resilience. They balance structure and flexibility. Health becomes not a private burden but a shared priority.

3. Joy

Joy is often undervalued in discussions of responsibility, yet it is essential to flourishing. Families that cultivate joy:

- create rituals and shared experiences,
- celebrate milestones and small victories,
- encourage playfulness and humor, and
- protect time for leisure and shared recreation.

Joy strengthens bonds. It reinforces the idea that life together is not merely functional but meaningful.

4. Kindness

Kindness shapes the family's moral climate. It shapes how differences are handled and how power is exercised. In flourishing families:

- Members speak respectfully, even in disagreement.
- Adults model apologies and repair.
- Generosity toward others is encouraged.
- Empathy is explicitly taught and practiced.

Kindness does not eliminate conflict. It transforms how conflict unfolds.

5. Learning

Families are lifelong learning environments. A flourishing family culture embraces curiosity and growth. It treats mistakes as opportunities for learning rather than as sources of shame.

This includes:

- Encouraging questions and exploration
- Modeling intellectual humility
- Valuing education broadly—not just formal schooling
- Reflecting together on experiences

A learning-oriented family prepares its members to adapt to a changing world.

6. Connection

Connection is the thread that weaves flourishing values together. Flourishing families cultivate:

- regular shared time,
- emotional availability,
- attentive listening, and
- inclusion in decision-making.

Connection fosters belonging. Belonging supports confidence. Confidence enables contribution.

II. How Society Can Support Thriving Family Cultures

Families do not exist in isolation. They are nested within economic, political, and cultural systems that either reinforce or undermine their capacity to flourish.

If we want flourishing family cultures, society must provide conditions that sustain them.

1. Economic Stability

Financial insecurity strains family systems. Chronic stress erodes patience, reduces emotional availability, and heightens conflict. Policies that promote stable employment, living wages, accessible childcare, and affordable housing indirectly strengthen family cultures by lowering chronic stress.

2. Work-Life Integration

When work structures demand constant availability or excessive hours, family connections erode. Flexible scheduling, parental leave, and predictable hours help families sustain rituals, shared meals, and meaningful engagement.

3. Accessible Health Care

Affordable physical and mental health care reduces stigma and prevents minor struggles from escalating into crises that destabilize family life.

4. Educational Partnerships

Schools that partner with families—rather than replace or marginalize them—reinforce shared learning values. Parent education resources can help caregivers intentionally foster flourishing norms at home.

5. Community Infrastructure

Safe public spaces, parks, recreational facilities, community organizations, and cultural institutions provide families with opportunities for connection and shared joy.

6. Cultural Narratives

Media and public discourse shape expectations for family life. When narratives emphasize competition, perfectionism, or material success alone, families may feel pressured and compare themselves to one another. When narratives highlight kindness, contribution, and resilience, families are supported in cultivating those values.

Society strengthens itself when it recognizes that supporting families is not a private charity but a public investment.

III. Assessing Flourishing in Families

To cultivate flourishing, we must be able to observe it. Assessment need not be intrusive or rigid. It can serve as a reflective inquiry.

A flourishing family assessment might examine:

A. Shared Values Alignment

- Are productive work, health, joy, kindness, learning, and connection regularly discussed or modeled?
- Do family members understand what the family stands for?

B. Emotional Climate

- Is there psychological safety?
- Can disagreements occur without humiliation or intimidation?
- Is repair practiced after conflict?

C. Structural Support

- Are routines predictable enough to provide stability?
- Is time protected for connection and rest?

D. Opportunity and Growth

- Do members feel encouraged to pursue their goals?
- Are efforts recognized and celebrated?

E. External Stressors

- Are financial pressures overwhelming?
- Is work-life balance sustainable?
- Does the broader environment support or strain family cohesion?

Assessment may include periodic family conversations, brief self-reflection questionnaires, or facilitated dialogue. The purpose is not grading but awareness. Awareness enables adjustment. Adjustment enables growth.

Families as Cultural Engines

Families transmit more than genetics. They pass on expectations, habits, and hope. They are small cultures that ripple outward into neighborhoods, schools, workplaces, and governments.

When family cultures normalize dignity, effort, health, joy, kindness, learning, and connection, those values echo throughout society. When families are chronically strained, fragmented, or unsupported, the effects reverberate just as widely.

A flourishing society, therefore, begins at the level of daily interactions—how we speak at the dinner table, how we divide responsibilities, how we respond to mistakes, how we celebrate, and how we repair.

Families do not need to be perfect to flourish. They need alignment, support, and intentionality.

When families are supported in cultivating cultures of contribution and care, society gains citizens who are more resilient, empathetic, capable, and connected. From such families, a flourishing society becomes not merely an aspiration—but a lived possibility.

Chapter 11

The Role of Educational Institutions in a Flourishing Society

EDUCATIONAL INSTITUTIONS PLAY a foundational role in shaping both individual development and collective capacity. In a flourishing society, education is understood not merely as credentialing or workforce preparation but as the cultivation of human potential across cognitive, emotional, social, and ethical dimensions.

This chapter addresses the full span of educational institutions—from early childhood settings through higher education. While much of its focus is on K–12 schooling, where foundational habits of mind and character are first formed, the same framework applies to colleges and universities as well. Higher education institutions do more than credential graduates: they serve as centers of research and discovery, generate and disseminate ideas that shape cultural norms and policy, and attract global talent that strengthens both economic vitality and cultural richness. A flourishing higher education culture—one that models intellectual humility, civic engagement, and genuine inquiry—sends graduates into every sector of society carrying those values with them.

Educational institutions are among the most influential cultural environments in any society. Schools do more than transmit knowledge. They shape identity, reinforce norms, distribute opportunities, cultivate habits of mind, and influence how young people understand work, health, belonging, and contribution.

If families are the first cultural ecosystem, schools are the first large-scale social ecosystem most individuals encounter. They are where diverse individuals learn to cooperate beyond kinship. For that reason, the culture of educational institutions has profound implications for a society's long-term flourishing.

A flourishing society depends not only on high-performing schools but also on healthy school cultures—cultures that intentionally embody values such as productive work, health, joy, kindness, learning, and connection. This chapter examines how educational institutions can embody those values; what conditions broader society must create to support thriving educational cultures; how flourishing in schools can be meaningfully assessed; and how a flourishing societal culture helps educational institutions achieve their own deepest goals.

Healthy school cultures:

- cultivate curiosity, critical thinking, and a love of learning,
- support well-being and belonging alongside academic growth,
- teach cooperation, conflict navigation, and civic responsibility, and
- recognize diverse abilities and learning styles.

I. Embodying Flourishing Values in School Culture

School culture is expressed through leadership signals, peer norms, classroom practices, reward systems, and daily routines. It is reflected not only in mission statements but also in what is encouraged, modeled, and reinforced.

1. Productive Work

In flourishing educational institutions, work is framed as meaningful effort rather than mere compliance. Students are encouraged to see themselves as contributors—active participants in learning rather than passive recipients.

A flourishing school culture supports productive work by:

- emphasizing mastery and growth over rank and comparison,
- recognizing effort, improvement, and perseverance,
- encouraging collaborative problem-solving, and
- connecting academic work to real-world contributions.

Teachers, too, are treated as professionals engaged in purposeful work. When faculty feel respected and supported, they model engagement and intrinsic motivation for students.

Productive work in education fosters competence, agency, and long-term resilience.

2. Health

Health in schools encompasses physical safety, mental well-being, and emotional climate. A flourishing educational institution:

- promotes physical activity and adequate rest,
- provides access to mental health support,
- reduces unnecessary stressors, and
- fosters psychological safety in classrooms.

Students learn best when anxiety is not overwhelming. Chronic stress narrows attention and impairs learning. By contrast, supportive environments broaden cognitive bandwidth and strengthen executive functioning.

Faculty health matters equally. Burned-out educators cannot sustain thriving learning cultures. Schools that prioritize workload, collegial support, and professional growth create conditions for long-term vitality.

3. Joy

Joy is not frivolous in education; it is a catalyst for curiosity and engagement. Flourishing schools:

- celebrate discovery,
- protect time for creativity and play,
- integrate arts, music, and movement, and
- recognize milestones and collective achievements.

Joy strengthens intrinsic motivation. It builds positive associations with learning and deepens the connection among students and staff.

4. Kindness

Kindness shapes the moral climate of educational institutions. It influences how differences are handled, how discipline is applied, and how authority is exercised.

Flourishing schools cultivate kindness by:

- modeling respectful communication,
- teaching empathy and perspective-taking,
- addressing conflict through restorative practices, and
- protecting vulnerable students from exclusion or bullying.

Kindness does not mean permissiveness. It means firmness paired with dignity. It builds trust and reduces fear-based compliance.

5. Learning

Learning is both the purpose and the means of flourishing in education. In thriving school cultures:

- curiosity is encouraged,
- mistakes are framed as opportunities,
- critical thinking is valued, and
- intellectual humility is modeled.

Learning extends beyond test performance. It encompasses social-emotional development, ethical reasoning, and civic understanding. Schools that foster lifelong learners strengthen society's adaptive capacity.

6. Connection

Connection strengthens the educational ecosystem. Flourishing schools cultivate:

- strong teacher-student relationships,
- collaborative peer cultures,
- family-school partnerships, and
- faculty collegiality.

When students feel known and valued, engagement increases; when teachers feel supported, innovation flourishes. When families are welcomed as partners, trust deepens.

Connection is the relational infrastructure of effective learning.

II. How Society Can Support Thriving Educational Cultures

Educational institutions do not operate in isolation. They reflect and respond to broader economic, political, and cultural pressures.

To foster flourishing schools, we must create enabling conditions.

1. Stable and Sufficient Funding

Under-resourced schools struggle to sustain health, joy, and connection. Sufficient funding ensures access to qualified educators, enrichment opportunities, safe facilities, and mental health services.

Investing in education is not merely a budget line; it is a long-term strategy for building societal capacity.

1a. Sufficient Resources as a Structural Commitment

Equitable funding is necessary but not sufficient. In most societies, school quality is deeply stratified by race, class, and geography—a structural reality that flourishing rhetoric alone cannot address. Students in under-resourced schools do not merely receive fewer enrichment opportunities; they often encounter higher levels of chronic stress, less experienced teaching staff, deteriorating facilities, and reduced access to mental health support. These are not individual misfortunes; they are systemic patterns that compound across generations.

A flourishing society confronts this directly. It recognizes that a school system which cultivates flourishing for some students while leaving others behind has not achieved flourishing—it has achieved a more comfortable inequality. Equity is not a supplement to the flourishing framework; it is a precondition of it. Closing opportunity gaps requires sustained investment, political will, and accountability systems that make disparities visible rather than obscuring them behind aggregate averages.

2. Balanced Accountability Systems

Excessive focus on narrow performance metrics can distort school culture. When test scores dominate evaluation, creativity, joy, and relational learning may erode.

Balanced accountability recognizes multiple dimensions of student development—academic, social, emotional, and civic. This tension is one of the deepest in contemporary education, and it deserves more than a policy footnote. Schools are simultaneously asked to be egalitarian and excellent, nurturing and rigorous, accountable and autonomous—and these demands frequently conflict. A flourishing society does not resolve this tension by pretending it does not exist. It builds accountability systems sophisticated enough to hold schools responsible for the full range of outcomes that matter: civic readiness, social-emotional development, and the cultivation of curiosity alongside academic mastery. Where those systems do not yet exist, creating them is among the most important investments a society can make in its educational institutions.

3. *Professional Respect for Educators*

Teachers and administrators need autonomy, professional development, and reasonable workloads. Respect for educators boosts morale and reduces turnover, stabilizing school culture. But teacher agency goes deeper than workload management. Teachers are the primary builders of school culture—not merely recipients of good conditions but active shapers of the values, habits, and relationships that define a school's character. A flourishing school treats its teachers as professionals with judgment worth trusting: involving them in curriculum decisions, honoring their observations about students, and creating space for them to adapt and innovate rather than execute prescribed programs. When teachers feel genuinely respected—not just supported—they are far more likely to extend that same respect to their students. The culture flows downward from how institutions treat the adults within them.

4. *Family and Community Partnerships*

Policies that promote collaboration between schools and families foster shared responsibility for learning. Community engagement programs, after-school initiatives, and mentorship networks expand the learning ecosystem.

5. Integration of Health Services

Accessible mental health and wellness services in schools reduce barriers to support and prevent challenges from escalating into crises.

6. Cultural Narratives About Education

Public discourse shapes expectations. When society frames education solely as economic competition, pressure intensifies. When education is framed as human development and civic preparation, flourishing becomes central.

Supporting educational institutions requires recognizing that they are cultural engines, not merely instructional sites.

III. Assessing Flourishing in Educational Institutions

To cultivate flourishing, educational leaders must be able to observe and measure it thoughtfully. Assessment should go beyond academic output to include cultural and relational indicators. A comprehensive assessment of flourishing in schools might examine the following domains and indicators:

A. Shared Values Alignment

- The extent to which productive work, health, joy, kindness, learning, and connection are visibly integrated into school policies, routines, and practices
- The clarity and consistency with which the school's guiding values are communicated
- The degree to which students and staff can articulate and demonstrate those values in daily interactions

B. Emotional and Social Climate

- Students' reported sense of safety, belonging, and respect
- Trends in bullying, exclusion, or disciplinary incidents
- Evidence of psychological safety in classrooms, including openness to questions and mistakes
- The quality of conflict resolution and restorative practices

C. Engagement and Motivation

- Levels of student engagement and intrinsic motivation in learning activities
- Student participation in collaborative and project-based learning
- Teacher-reported professional satisfaction, support, and autonomy
- Indicators of sustained attention, curiosity, and perseverance

D. Health and Well-Being Indicators

- Student attendance and chronic absenteeism rates
- Staff burnout, retention, and turnover rates
- Utilization and accessibility of counseling and support services
- Measures of workload balance and stress levels among students and staff

E. Growth and Opportunity Indicators

- Academic progress across diverse student populations
- Reduction of achievement gaps

- Access to enrichment opportunities (arts, athletics, advanced coursework, service learning)
- Student participation in civic engagement and community service

F. Relational Strength Indicators

- Quality and stability of teacher-student relationships
- Levels of peer collaboration and mutual support
- Family participation and partnership in school activities
- Collegial collaboration, trust, and shared problem-solving among faculty

Assessment tools may include climate surveys, focus groups, performance data, and observations from classroom visits. The goal is not to reduce flourishing to numbers but to foster informed reflection that guides improvement.

IV. How a Flourishing Societal Culture Supports Educational Institutions

The relationship between educational institutions and society is reciprocal. Schools shape society, but society also shapes what schools can become. A flourishing societal culture does not merely set expectations for schools—it actively creates the conditions under which schools can achieve their deepest goals.

What are those goals? At their core, educational institutions seek to cultivate curious, capable, and ethical people; to expand opportunity regardless of background; to transmit and renew the knowledge and values a society depends on; and to prepare young people not just to navigate the world as it is but to improve it. A flourishing societal culture actively advances each of these goals in ways that no school policy alone can replicate.

When the broader culture values learning over credentialing, students arrive at school already understanding that curiosity matters—and teachers are freed from the exhausting task of convincing them. When society models intellectual humility in its public discourse, schools find it easier to teach students that changing one's mind is a sign of strength. When communities normalize kindness and constructive conflict, schools spend less energy managing hostility and more energy cultivating genuine collaboration.

A flourishing culture also elevates the status of educators. In societies that genuinely honor teaching as a vocation—rather than treating it as a residual choice for those who could not pursue more prestigious careers—schools attract and retain people of exceptional talent and commitment. The cultural narrative surrounding teaching is not incidental; it directly shapes who enters the profession and how long they stay.

Finally, a flourishing societal culture makes providing adequate resources not just a policy goal but a shared moral commitment. When citizens broadly believe that every child deserves a genuinely excellent education—and hold their institutions accountable to that belief—schools are supported in doing the difficult, long-term work of closing opportunity gaps. That support cannot be manufactured solely within schools. It must be cultivated in the society around them.

Educational Institutions as Cultural Architects

Schools shape how future citizens understand work, differences, authority, cooperation, and possibility. They can reinforce competition and anxiety—or cultivate contribution and resilience. They can also magnify inequity—or expand opportunity.

When educational institutions intentionally embrace productive work, health, joy, kindness, learning, and connection, they do more than educate individuals. They strengthen society's moral and cognitive infrastructure.

A flourishing society depends on schools that not only prepare students to succeed within existing systems but also equip them to improve those systems.

When educational cultures are healthy, the ripple effects span generations. When society invests in thriving schools, it invests in its own future capacity to flourish.

Chapter 12

The Role of Workplaces in a Flourishing Society

FOR MANY ADULTS, workplaces are among the most influential institutions in daily life. For many people, work occupies more waking hours than family or community life. It shapes daily rhythms, stress levels, social networks, identity, and long-term opportunities—making workplaces one of the most consequential cultural environments most adults will ever inhabit.

Because of this, workplaces are not merely economic engines; they are cultural ecosystems. They shape how people experience productive effort, recognition, belonging, health, and purpose. A flourishing society, therefore, depends on flourishing workplace cultures—environments that strengthen human capacity rather than deplete it. This chapter argues that treating people well is not in tension with organizational performance—it is the most reliable path to it. Engaged employees outperform disengaged ones. Low-turnover organizations outcompete high-turnover ones. Psychologically safe teams innovate more than fearful ones. The evidence is consistent: human flourishing and business success are not opposing forces to be traded off against each other. They are mutually reinforcing. Where genuine tensions do arise—between short-term profit pressures and long-term investment in people—the path forward is not to choose one over the other but to design strategies that make flourishing the driver of sustainable competitive advantage.

Workplace culture is expressed through leadership behavior, peer norms, incentive systems, performance expectations, communication patterns, and daily routines. It is revealed not in slogans but in what is consistently rewarded, tolerated, and modeled.

In a flourishing society, workplaces intentionally embody the values of productive work, health, joy, kindness, learning, and connection. This chapter examines how workplaces can embody those values; what conditions broader society must create to support thriving workplace cultures; how flourishing at work can be meaningfully assessed; and how a flourishing societal culture helps workplaces achieve their own deepest goals.

A candid note on power is warranted here. Workplaces are among the primary contexts in modern life where power asymmetries are most consequential. Employers set wages, hours, conditions, and terms of continued employment. Employees, particularly those without specialized skills or union protections, often have limited recourse when those conditions fall short. This chapter does not treat flourishing workplaces as a matter of good intentions alone. It recognizes that structural conditions—policy, regulation, and market incentives—shape what is possible, and that the responsibility for creating flourishing workplace cultures is shared between individual organizations and the broader society in which they operate.

I. Embodying Flourishing Values in Workplace Culture

1. Productive Work

Productive work is central to human dignity. In flourishing workplaces, productivity is framed not as relentless output but as meaningful contribution.

Thriving workplace cultures:

- clarify purpose and align roles with a larger mission,
- align incentives with long-term value creation,
- recognize effort, improvement, and collaboration, and
- encourage autonomy and ownership.

Employees who understand how their work matters are more engaged, resilient, and innovative. Well-structured, productive work strengthens both organizational performance and personal growth.

2. Health

Workplace health encompasses physical safety, mental well-being, and a manageable workload.

Flourishing workplaces:

- promote reasonable workload expectations,
- support work-life integration,
- provide access to mental health resources,
- reduce chronic stressors whenever possible, and
- encourage restorative breaks and boundaries.

Chronic stress narrows attention and raises error rates. Sustainable performance requires environments that replenish energy rather than deplete it.

Employee health is a fundamental human right and one of the most powerful drivers of sustained organizational performance. These two facts are not in conflict. Protecting health is both an ethical choice and a strategic one. Unsafe working conditions must be addressed. Organizations that invest in employee well-being reduce absenteeism, lower turnover costs, and unlock the discretionary effort that distinguishes good performance from excellent performance.

3. Joy

Joy in the workplace may seem secondary to results, yet it is crucial to engagement and creativity.

Thriving organizations:

- celebrate milestones and achievements,
- encourage humor and positive social interactions,
- provide opportunities for creativity and innovation, and
- recognize individual strengths.

Joy enhances motivation and strengthens team cohesion. It fosters discretionary effort and reduces turnover.

4. Kindness

Kindness shapes the workplace's moral climate. It influences how authority is exercised, how feedback is delivered, and how mistakes are addressed.

In flourishing workplaces:

- communication is respectful and direct,
- feedback is constructive rather than humiliating,
- leaders model empathy and fairness, and
- conflicts are addressed promptly and thoughtfully.

Kindness does not eliminate accountability. It ensures accountability is upheld with dignity. Trust grows where kindness and competence coexist.

5. Learning

Adaptive capacity is essential in modern economies. Flourishing workplaces embrace continuous learning.

This includes:

- Professional development opportunities
- Psychological safety for experimentation
- Viewing mistakes as learning opportunities
- Cross-functional collaboration

Learning-oriented cultures innovate more effectively and respond more resiliently to change. They prepare organizations—and the society they serve—for future challenges.

6. Connection

Connection is the relational infrastructure of effective workplaces.

Thriving organizations cultivate:

- strong team cohesion,
- cross-level communication,
- inclusive decision-making when appropriate, and
- a shared sense of purpose.

Employees who feel known and valued show greater commitment and lower disengagement. Connection reduces isolation and strengthens collaboration.

II. How Society Can Support Thriving Workplace Cultures

Workplaces operate within broader economic and policy frameworks. If society seeks flourishing workplace cultures, structural conditions must support them.

1. Economic Stability and Fair Compensation

Living wages, predictable scheduling, and fair labor practices reduce chronic stress and strengthen employee engagement. Financial insecurity outside work inevitably undermines performance at work.

2. Balanced Regulatory Frameworks

Labor protections, health and safety standards, and anti-discrimination laws establish a baseline of dignity. These guardrails allow organizations to innovate without undermining human well-being.

3. Incentives for Long-Term Value Creation

When capital markets prioritize short-term returns, workplace cultures often lean toward overwork and extraction. Incentive structures that reward sustainable growth foster healthier workplaces. This is one of the most structurally important levers available. Quarterly earnings pressure is not merely an abstract financial concern—it directly shapes how managers treat employees. When leaders are rewarded for this quarter's numbers and penalized for investments whose returns take years to materialize, the result is predictable: training budgets are cut, benefits are trimmed, workloads are pushed beyond sustainable limits, and the very conditions that produce long-term performance are sacrificed for short-term optics. A flourishing society creates governance structures—through reporting requirements, executive compensation reform, and long-term investment incentives—that make it easier for businesses to act on what the evidence already shows: that investing in people is the highest-return strategy available to most organizations over a five- to ten-year horizon.

4. Supportive Environments Within Workplaces

Workplace flourishing is not distributed. In most organizations, the experience of productive work, health, joy, kindness, learning, and connection varies considerably by race, gender, class, and job level. A senior manager and a frontline worker at the same company may inhabit cultures so different that they can barely be said to work in the same place. The manager experiences autonomy, recognition, and opportunities for development; the worker experiences surveillance, unpredictable scheduling, and minimal recourse when treated unfairly. A chapter on workplace flourishing that does not acknowledge this is describing some employees' experiences as if they were the experiences of all.

A flourishing workplace is one where these values are not reserved for those at the top of the hierarchy. It actively works to extend psychological safety, growth opportunities, fair compensation, and dignity to every level of the organization. This is not only an ethical imperative—it is a competitive one. Organizations that focus on flourishing at the top while tolerating poor conditions at the bottom suffer the consequences: high frontline turnover, disengagement, reputational damage, and the loss of institutional knowledge carried by experienced workers. Supportive work environments retain talent, reduce costly churn, and build the trust that makes sustained high performance possible.

5. Access to Health and Childcare Support

Affordable health care, parental leave policies, and access to childcare enable employees to balance professional and family responsibilities without chronic strain.

6. Education and Workforce Development

Partnerships between educational institutions and employers ensure that skill development remains aligned with evolving economic needs. Lifelong learning infrastructure strengthens individuals and workplaces alike.

7. *Cultural Narratives About Work*

Public discourse shapes expectations. When work is framed solely as status competition, stress intensifies; when it is framed as contribution and collaborative problem-solving, dignity and meaning increase.

Society reinforces workplace flourishing by valuing long-term human development alongside economic output.

III. Assessing Flourishing in Workplaces

Intentional cultures require intentional measurement. Assessing flourishing in workplaces entails evaluating cultural alignment, relational strength, and the sustainability of performance.

A flourishing workplace assessment framework might include:

A. Shared Values Alignment

- The extent to which productive work, health, joy, kindness, learning, and connection are reflected in policies and daily practices
- Clarity of organizational purpose
- Alignment between stated values and actual reward systems

B. Emotional and Social Climate

- Employee perceptions of psychological safety
- Trust in leadership
- Incidence of harassment or unresolved conflict
- Sense of belonging across diverse employee groups

C. Engagement and Motivation

- Employee engagement survey results
- Discretionary effort indicators

- Voluntary turnover rates
- Internal mobility and advancement rates

D. Health and Sustainability Indicators

- Burnout and stress measures
- Sick leave and absenteeism trends
- Workload distribution patterns
- Utilization of wellness resources

E. Growth and Learning Indicators

- Participation in professional development
- Innovation metrics and idea generation
- Skill acquisition and career progression

F. Relational Strength Indicators

- Team collaboration scores
- Cross-departmental coordination
- Quality of supervisor-employee relationships
- Mentorship participation

Assessment tools may include climate surveys, turnover analytics, focus groups, performance data, and structured reflection sessions. The purpose is continuous improvement, not compliance.

IV. How a Flourishing Societal Culture Supports Workplaces

Workplaces do not operate in a cultural vacuum. The norms, expectations, and values that employees bring through the door each morning are shaped by the society around them. A flourishing societal culture does not merely demand better workplaces—it creates the conditions that make building them far more achievable.

What do workplaces most deeply seek to achieve? Beyond profit, most organizations—when asked candidly—describe goals that sound remarkably like flourishing: to attract and retain talented people who are motivated and committed; to build teams that solve hard problems creatively; to sustain performance over years and decades rather than quarters; to earn the trust of customers, communities, and employees. A flourishing societal culture supports every one of these goals.

When the broader culture normalizes learning and intellectual curiosity, employees arrive already oriented toward growth—reducing the cost of developing talent internally. When society models constructive conflict and honest communication, workplaces spend less energy managing defensive dynamics and more energy on creative problem-solving. When communities cultivate resilience and purpose, employees bring those capacities to work, strengthening team cohesion under pressure.

A flourishing culture also recalibrates what employees expect of their workplaces—and what workplaces expect of themselves. When society broadly communicates that dignity, fairness, and human development are non-negotiable features of any legitimate workplace, organizations face greater social pressure to deliver on those expectations. Reputational accountability in a flourishing society is real: employers who treat their people well attract talent; those who do not find themselves at a growing competitive disadvantage.

Finally, a flourishing societal culture addresses the most common objection leaders raise when asked to invest more in their people: that competitors will not follow and that the first mover will be at a disadvantage. When flourishing becomes a broadly shared expectation—reinforced by cultural norms, policy, and market demand—it ceases to be a unilateral sacrifice and becomes the standard. In such a society, treating people well is not a competitive risk. It is the price of admission to the talent market, and the foundation of any strategy worth sustaining.

Workplaces as Engines of Cultural Influence

Workplaces influence not only economic output but also societal norms. They shape how people understand authority, collaboration, fairness, and contribution. The patterns learned at work often spill into families, communities, and civic life.

When workplace cultures reinforce dignity, resilience, learning, and connection, they strengthen the broader social fabric. When they normalize chronic stress, inequity, or fear-based management, they erode it.

A flourishing society requires workplaces that balance performance with humanity—organizations that recognize that long-term prosperity depends on sustained human capacity.

When work strengthens rather than drains those who perform it, flourishing becomes not only an aspiration but a daily experience woven into the fabric of economic life.

Chapter 13

The Role of Civic and Community Organizations in a Flourishing Society

BETWEEN THE INTIMACY of families and the scale of national institutions lies a vital layer of social life: civic and community organizations. These include neighborhood associations, volunteer groups, faith communities, service clubs, cultural organizations, youth programs, advocacy groups, mutual aid networks, professional associations, and nonprofit organizations.

They are the connective tissue of society.

Civic and community organizations create spaces where individuals gather not primarily as consumers or employees but as participants. They foster belonging beyond kinship and economic exchange. In doing so, they strengthen trust, cooperation, and shared purpose—essential ingredients of a flourishing society.

When these organizations cultivate healthy cultures, they amplify the values of productive work, health, joy, kindness, learning, and connection in deeply practical ways. This chapter examines how civic and community organizations can embody those values; what conditions broader society must create to support thriving civic cultures; how flourishing within them can be meaningfully assessed; and how a flourishing societal culture helps civic organizations achieve their own deepest goals.

A candid accounting of civic life requires acknowledging its shadow as well as its promise. Civic organizations can also serve as vehicles for exclusion, factionalism, and the entrenchment of existing power. Neighborhood associations that resist affordable housing, advocacy groups organized around hostility to outsiders, and civic bodies captured by narrow interests are not aberrations—they are recurring patterns. The same organizing capacity that enables communities to solve shared problems can be directed toward protecting privilege or marginalizing those who are different. This chapter does not treat civic flourishing as automatic or inevitable. It recognizes that the values described here must be actively cultivated and continuously defended, and that a flourishing society attends to the quality of its civic institutions, not merely their quantity.

I. Embodying Flourishing Values in Civic and Community Organizations

Leadership behavior, volunteer norms, decision-making processes, communication patterns, and shared rituals shape civic culture. It is expressed in the way members are welcomed, conflicts are handled, and contributions are recognized.

1. Productive Work

Civic organizations channel energy into collective contributions. In flourishing civic cultures:

- members understand the mission and see how their efforts matter,

- volunteer roles are clear and meaningful,
- effort is recognized and appreciated, and
- outcomes are measured by impact, not just activity.

Productive work in civic settings strengthens agency and reinforces the belief that individuals can shape their communities. It fosters civic confidence—the conviction that participation makes a difference.

2. *Health*

Civic organizations contribute to community and individual health.

Flourishing civic cultures:

- avoid burnout by distributing responsibilities sustainably,
- create psychologically safe environments for participation,
- offer supportive networks during personal or community crises, and
- encourage balance between service and self-care.

Because many civic organizations rely on volunteer energy, attention to sustainable engagement is essential. Chronic overextension can erode morale and reduce impact.

Healthy civic organizations strengthen community resilience.

3. *Joy*

Joy binds people together and sustains long-term engagement.

Thriving civic groups:

- celebrate shared accomplishments,
- integrate rituals, events, and social gatherings,
- encourage humor and positive connection, and
- recognize milestones and contributions.

Joy transforms obligation into belonging. It turns participation from a duty into shared meaning.

4. Kindness

Kindness shapes the moral tone of civic life.

In flourishing civic organizations:

- disagreements are handled respectfully,
- diversity of perspectives is welcomed,
- new members are actively included and supported, and
- leaders model humility and fairness.

Kindness builds trust and reduces factionalism. It makes civic engagement inviting rather than intimidating.

5. Learning

Civic organizations are powerful learning environments that transmit civic knowledge, organizational skills, and cultural norms.

Flourishing civic cultures:

- encourage dialogue and reflection,
- provide leadership development opportunities,
- share best practices and lessons learned, and
- remain open to innovation.

Learning strengthens adaptability and long-term effectiveness.

6. Connection

Connection is the central contribution to civic life.

Civic and community organizations:

- build bridges across age, profession, culture, and ideology,
- foster intergenerational exchange,
- create a shared identity around common goals, and
- reduce social isolation.

In an era marked by fragmentation and digital distance, face-to-face civic connection is especially valuable. It strengthens social trust—the invisible infrastructure that underpins flourishing societies. Social trust—the generalized confidence that others can be relied upon and that institutions act in good faith—is not a given. It is cultivated through repeated experiences of cooperation across differences. Research consistently shows that participation in civic organizations is among the strongest predictors of interpersonal trust, and that declining civic participation tracks closely with declining social trust across many societies. Reversing that decline requires not only preserving existing civic institutions but actively creating the conditions for new ones to form and take root.

The digital dimension of civic connection deserves direct attention. Online organizing, digital mutual aid networks, and social media-based advocacy have transformed how civic life is conducted. At their best, digital platforms lower barriers to participation, enable communities separated by geography to act collectively, and give voice to those who might be excluded from traditional civic structures. At their worst, they accelerate factionalism, reward outrage over deliberation, and create the illusion of connection without its substance. A flourishing civic culture uses digital tools intentionally—harnessing their reach while investing in the face-to-face encounters where trust is most durably built.

II. How Society Can Support Thriving Civic and Community Organizations

Civic organizations do not flourish in isolation. Their vitality depends on broader structural conditions.

1. Supportive Legal and Regulatory Environments

Clear, fair nonprofit regulations, transparent reporting systems, and reasonable administrative requirements enable organizations to focus on their mission rather than on compliance burdens.

2. Sustainable Funding Mechanisms

Access to grants, philanthropic partnerships, and community fundraising opportunities supports long-term planning. Excessive financial instability can undermine continuity and trust.

3. Public Recognition of Civic Contribution

Cultural narratives that value volunteerism and civic participation foster engagement. When society honors service, more people step forward.

4. Infrastructure and Shared Spaces

Community centers, public libraries, parks, and digital platforms provide gathering spaces that reduce barriers to participation.

5. Leadership Development Pathways

Training programs and mentorship networks strengthen governance capacity and succession planning in civic organizations.

6. Cross-Sector Collaboration

Partnerships among government, businesses, schools, and nonprofits can multiply impact. When civic organizations are treated as essential partners rather than peripheral actors, their effectiveness grows. But genuine partnership is distinct from superficial inclusion. Civic organizations are sometimes invited to the table only after decisions have been made—consulted for legitimacy rather than listened to for insight. Genuine cross-sector collaboration means sharing not only credit but decision-making authority; not only resources but risk. Governments that contract with civic organizations while imposing burdensome reporting requirements, dictating program design, or treating community knowledge as less valid than professional expertise are not partners—they are employers. A flourishing society cultivates the kind of institutional humility that allows civic organizations to lead, not merely to implement.

Supporting civic organizations is not charity; it is an investment in social cohesion and democratic capacity.

III. Assessing Flourishing in Civic and Community Organizations

A flourishing culture does not sustain itself without thoughtful examination. A flourishing assessment framework for civic organizations might consider the following domains:

A. Shared Values Alignment

- Clarity of mission and purpose
- Alignment between stated values and daily practices
- Member understanding of organizational goals

B. Emotional and Social Climate

- Member sense of belonging and inclusion
- Psychological safety in meetings and discussions
- Respectful handling of disagreements
- Diversity and representation within leadership and membership

C. Engagement and Participation

- Volunteer retention rates
- Active participation levels
- Leadership pipeline development
- Member satisfaction and motivation

D. Health and Sustainability

- Distribution of workload among members
- Risk of volunteer burnout
- Financial stability and transparency
- Succession planning for leadership roles

E. Growth and Learning

- Opportunities for skill development
- Responsiveness to community feedback
- Adaptation to changing community needs
- Evidence of program improvement over time

F. Relational Strength

- Partnerships with other organizations
- Community trust and reputation
- Cross-demographic engagement
- Frequency and quality of collaborative initiatives

Assessment tools may include member surveys, structured reflection sessions, community feedback, impact data, and governance reviews. The goal is not bureaucratic complexity but continuous alignment with flourishing values.

IV. How a Flourishing Societal Culture Supports Civic and Community Organizations

The relationship between civic organizations and the societies they inhabit is reciprocal. Civic organizations strengthen society—but a flourishing societal culture also actively sustains them, providing the conditions for them to achieve their deepest purposes.

What do civic organizations most seek to achieve? At their core, they seek to build community—to create a sense of belonging, shared purpose, and mutual care that allow people to face challenges together rather than alone. They seek to give individuals a meaningful role in shaping the conditions of their own lives. They seek to sustain the habits of democratic participation across generations. A flourishing societal culture does not merely tolerate these goals—it actively enables them.

When the broader culture values civic participation—when volunteering is honored rather than treated as a secondary pursuit, when community service is recognized alongside professional achievement, when local leadership is celebrated as a genuine vocation—civic organizations attract more people with greater commitment. The cultural narrative surrounding civic life is not incidental; it directly shapes who shows up and how long they stay.

A flourishing societal culture also models the civic virtues that organizations depend on to function well: the willingness to engage with those who hold different views, the patience to work through disagreements rather than retreat from them, and the capacity to hold shared purpose alongside personal differences. When these virtues are degraded in public life—when political discourse normalizes contempt, and when winning becomes more important than working together—civic organizations struggle to maintain the trust and generosity that make them effective. The health of civic organizations mirrors the health of the society around them.

Finally, a flourishing societal culture invests materially in civic capacity—not because civic organizations are efficient service-delivery mechanisms but because the process of people coming together to address shared concerns is itself a social good, independent of any particular outcome. The relationships formed, the skills developed, and the trust built through civic participation are not byproducts of the work. They are among its most important products. A society that understands this invests in civic infrastructure the way it invests in schools and roads: as foundational to everything else.

Civic Life as the Heartbeat of Flourishing

Civic and community organizations are where strangers become neighbors, where shared concerns become shared action, and where individual capacity becomes collective strength.

They cultivate the habits of cooperation, empathy, dialogue, and contribution that sustain democratic life. When civic cultures embrace productive work, health, joy, kindness, learning, and connection, they reinforce these values across society.

A flourishing society depends not only on strong markets and effective governments but on vibrant civic life. When people gather freely to solve problems, celebrate culture, and support one another, they strengthen the bonds that make collective flourishing possible.

Civic and community organizations are not peripheral to societal well-being. They are its living expression. In an era of declining trust, rising isolation, and deepening polarization, the stakes of that expression have rarely been higher. A society that allows its civic life to wither is not merely losing a pleasant amenity—it is losing the capacity to renew itself. Investing in the health of civic and community organizations is, ultimately, an investment in the possibility of flourishing itself.

Chapter 14

The Role of Healthcare in a Flourishing Society

HEALTHCARE OCCUPIES A unique place in society. It stands at the intersection of vulnerability and expertise, science and compassion, and crisis and prevention. When functioning well, healthcare does more than treat illness—it protects capacity, restores dignity, and strengthens resilience across communities.

In a flourishing society, healthcare extends beyond episodic intervention. It is integrated into a broader vision of human development. It supports not only survival but also vitality. It reinforces healthy lifestyle choices, preventive care, mental health, relational support, and long-term well-being.

Like other institutions, healthcare systems embody a culture. That culture is expressed in clinical norms, leadership behavior, workload expectations, communication patterns, incentive systems, and patient experience. When aligned with flourishing values—productive work, health, joy, kindness, learning, and connection—healthcare becomes a stabilizing force in society. This chapter examines how healthcare institutions can embody those values; what conditions broader society must create to support thriving healthcare cultures; how flourishing in healthcare can be meaningfully assessed; and how a flourishing societal culture helps healthcare achieve its own deepest goals.

A flourishing healthcare system is genuinely available to everyone. No vision of healthcare flourishing is complete if good care remains out of reach for large portions of the population—whether because of cost, geography, language, or the way services are organized. This is not primarily a political argument; it is a practical one. When people cannot access preventive care, minor conditions can become serious. When cost deters early treatment, the burden on families, communities, and the broader healthcare system grows. A flourishing society works to reduce every barrier between people and the care they need—making healthcare not a privilege contingent on circumstance but an opportunity available to all. Affordability, proximity, and accessibility are not peripheral concerns; they are the foundation on which everything else in this chapter depends.

I. Embodying Flourishing Values in Healthcare

1. Productive Work

Healthcare is deeply purposeful work. In flourishing healthcare systems, productivity is defined not merely by the volume of services delivered but by quality, outcomes, and patient well-being.

Thriving healthcare cultures:

- align incentives with long-term health outcomes,
- support interdisciplinary teamwork,
- recognize clinical judgment and professional expertise,
- reduce unnecessary administrative burden, and
- emphasize preventive and population health approaches.

When clinicians can focus on meaningful patient care rather than excessive bureaucracy, patient outcomes and professional satisfaction both improve.

2. Health

Health is the central mission of healthcare, but a flourishing healthcare system extends beyond treating disease to cultivate well-being.

A flourishing healthcare system:

- invests in preventive care and early intervention,
- integrates physical and mental health services,
- addresses social determinants of health,
- promotes health literacy, and
- supports lifestyle changes and resilience.

Health is understood as a shared endeavor between providers and patients. The goal is sustained vitality, not merely symptom management.

Internally, healthcare organizations must also protect providers' health. Burnout, compassion fatigue, and chronic overwork undermine both the quality of care and system stability.

3. Joy

Joy may seem distant from clinical settings, yet it is essential to sustaining compassionate care.

Flourishing healthcare cultures:

- celebrate patient recovery milestones,
- recognize team achievements,
- create space for gratitude and acknowledgment, and
- foster collegial warmth and mutual support.

Moments of joy reinforce meaning in demanding environments. They protect against emotional depletion and strengthen team cohesion.

4. Kindness

Kindness is foundational to healthcare. Patients often enter the system during moments of fear, pain, or uncertainty.

In flourishing healthcare environments:

- communication is clear and respectful,
- patients are treated as partners in care,
- cultural sensitivity is practiced,
- errors are addressed transparently, and
- colleagues support one another during high-stress situations.

Kindness does not diminish clinical rigor. It builds trust and improves adherence, satisfaction, and healing.

5. Learning

Healthcare depends on continuous learning. Scientific knowledge evolves rapidly, and systems must adapt.

A flourishing healthcare culture:

- encourages ongoing professional development,
- integrates evidence-based practice,
- promotes interdisciplinary case reviews,
- supports quality improvement initiatives, and
- learns from errors rather than concealing them.

Learning-oriented healthcare organizations improve outcomes and reduce preventable harm.

6. Connection

Connection operates at multiple levels in healthcare.

Flourishing healthcare fosters:

- strong provider-patient relationships,
- collaborative interdisciplinary teams,
- partnerships with families and caregivers, and
- integration with community organizations.

Connection reduces fragmentation, strengthens continuity of care, and enhances patient trust. At the societal level, healthcare institutions can serve as hubs of community stability.

II. How Society Can Support Thriving Healthcare Cultures

Healthcare organizations operate within policy, reimbursement, and regulatory environments that profoundly shape their culture.

If society seeks flourishing healthcare systems, supportive structures are essential.

1. Payment Models Aligned with Outcomes

Reimbursement systems that prioritize value over volume promote preventive care and long-term health outcomes rather than episodic interventions. This is one of the most consequential levers available to society, and it deserves more than a passing mention. In many healthcare systems, financial incentives are misaligned with human flourishing in ways that directly shape clinical culture: profitable procedures receive investment while unglamorous prevention is underfunded; conditions that affect wealthier patients attract research and resources while others languish; consolidation reduces patient choice and drives up costs without improving care. These are not incidental market failures—they are predictable consequences of financing structures that were not designed to foster flourishing. A flourishing society deliberately reforms those structures, shifting reimbursement toward outcomes, investing in primary and preventive care, and holding healthcare markets accountable for the accessibility and quality of what they deliver. The goal is a system in which doing right by patients and doing well as an organization are not competing imperatives but aligned ones.

2. *Workforce Investment*

Adequate staffing, training programs, and fair compensation reduce burnout and improve retention.

3. *Integration of Mental and Physical Health*

Policy frameworks that treat mental health as integral—not secondary—enhance overall well-being.

4. *Administrative Simplification*

Reducing unnecessary documentation and bureaucratic complexity enables clinicians to focus on patient care.

5. *Public Health Infrastructure*

Investment in public health systems strengthens preparedness and preventive capacity.

6. *Cultural Respect for Care Work*

Societal recognition of healthcare as skilled and compassionate work reinforces morale and attracts talent. This recognition is especially important for nurses, home health aides, medical assistants, and allied health workers, who form the backbone of daily care but are often underpaid and undervalued relative to their social contributions. A flourishing society closes the gap between what these roles are worth and what they receive in compensation, status, and working conditions that determine whether talented, caring people choose to stay in the profession.

7. Universal Access and Barrier Reduction

A healthcare system cannot truly flourish if large portions of the population cannot access it. Barriers come in many forms: costs that make care unaffordable, geography that makes care inaccessible, language and cultural differences that make care feel alienating, and administrative complexity that makes it exhausting to navigate. A flourishing society works systematically to remove each of these barriers—not through any single policy mechanism but through a sustained commitment to the principle that good healthcare should be genuinely available to everyone who needs it.

This means investing in community health infrastructure in underserved areas, supporting telehealth as a bridge to rural and isolated communities, training a diverse healthcare workforce that reflects the communities it serves, and designing care delivery systems around patients' needs rather than institutions' convenience. It also means addressing the upstream conditions that shape health in the first place: safe housing, nutritious food, clean air and water, opportunities for physical activity, and freedom from chronic stress. A healthcare system that treats people well when they arrive but ignores what made them sick in the first place is treating symptoms rather than causes. Expanding access to healthy living conditions is as much a healthcare strategy as expanding access to clinics.

Supporting healthcare organizations is not only about funding; it is about aligning incentives and expectations with long-term human flourishing.

III. Assessing Flourishing in Healthcare

Evaluating flourishing in healthcare requires attention to both patient outcomes and organizational culture.

A flourishing healthcare assessment framework might include:

A. Shared Values Alignment

- Clarity of mission focused on long-term health and dignity
- Alignment between stated values and clinical practice
- Patient understanding of care goals

B. Patient Experience and Trust

- Patient satisfaction and trust metrics
- Communication clarity
- Perceived respect and inclusion
- Complaint resolution processes

C. Clinical Outcomes and Preventive Indicators

- Population health metrics
- Preventive screening rates
- Chronic disease management outcomes
- Reduction in avoidable hospitalizations

D. Provider Well-Being

- Burnout rates
- Staff retention and turnover
- Workload distribution
- Access to mental health support for clinicians

E. Learning and Quality Improvement

- Participation in continuing education
- Implementation of evidence-based practices
- Quality improvement initiatives and outcomes
- Transparency in reporting safety data

F. Relational and System Integration

- Interdisciplinary collaboration
- Care coordination effectiveness
- Community partnerships
- Integration across levels of care

Assessment tools may include patient surveys, clinical dashboards, workforce analytics, peer review, and external audits. The purpose is not to create compliance burdens but to guide continuous alignment with flourishing values.

IV. How a Flourishing Societal Culture Supports Healthcare

Healthcare and society exist in a reciprocal relationship. Healthcare systems support society by maintaining the human capacity on which everything else depends. But a flourishing societal culture actively sustains healthcare in return, making it easier for healthcare institutions to achieve their deepest goals.

What does healthcare most deeply seek to achieve? Beyond treating illness, healthcare seeks to help people live well—to experience vitality, sustain relationships, pursue meaningful work, and face the inevitable challenges of illness and aging with dignity and support. A flourishing societal culture advances each of these goals in ways no clinical intervention alone can replicate.

When the broader culture normalizes health-promoting behaviors—adequate sleep, physical activity, nutritious eating, stress management—healthcare systems spend less time managing the consequences of preventable conditions and more time supporting genuine vitality. When society destigmatizes mental health challenges, people seek help earlier, reducing the severity of conditions that might otherwise go untreated for years. When communities are designed for walkability, access to green space, and social connection, the health benefits are measurable—and the burden on clinical care is meaningfully reduced.

A flourishing culture also elevates the status of caregiving as a vocation. When society genuinely honors those who dedicate their lives to healing others—not just in rhetoric but in compensation, working conditions, and social recognition—the healthcare workforce attracts and retains people of exceptional compassion and capability. The culture surrounding healthcare professions is not incidental; it directly shapes who enters them, how long they stay, and how much of themselves they bring to the work.

Finally, a flourishing societal culture treats access to good healthcare as a shared responsibility rather than an individual one. When people understand that their own health is connected to the health of those around them—that preventable illness in one household affects families, workplaces, schools, and communities—the political and social will to invest in accessible, high-quality care for everyone becomes easier to sustain. Healthcare flourishes most fully in a society that understands health itself as a commons: something we build and protect together, for the benefit of all.

Healthcare as Guardian of Human Capacity

Healthcare systems stand on the front lines of human vulnerability. They preserve life, restore function, and alleviate suffering. In a flourishing society, they do more. They strengthen long-term capacity—physical, emotional, and relational.

When healthcare organizations embody productive work, health, joy, kindness, learning, and connection, they reinforce these values across communities. They help individuals recover not only their bodies but also their sense of possibility.

A flourishing society depends on healthcare systems that treat patients with dignity, support clinicians sustainably, and align incentives with long-term well-being.

When care is delivered with competence and compassion, healthcare becomes not only a safety net but also a foundation for collective flourishing. When healthcare fails—when it is inaccessible, unaffordable, or organized around financial incentives rather than human need—the ripple effects reach far beyond the clinic. Families absorb the financial and emotional burden of untreated illness. Workplaces lose the sustained energy of healthy employees. Schools contend with children whose health needs go unmet. Civic life contracts when chronic illness and exhaustion leave people with too little capacity to participate. Healthcare is not a silo. It is woven into every other dimension of flourishing, and its failures are felt everywhere. That is why a flourishing society does not treat healthcare as a commodity to be rationed by circumstance. It treats it as a shared foundation—something every person deserves the opportunity to access, and something every institution depends upon to function at its best.

Chapter 15

The Role of Government in a Flourishing Society

GOVERNMENT IS AMONG the most powerful cultural architects in society. Through laws, policies, public investments, and institutional design, it shapes the incentives, norms, and opportunity structures that influence daily life. Government determines how rights are protected, how resources are allocated, how conflicts are resolved, and how collective priorities are expressed.

In a flourishing society, government is not merely a regulator or administrator. It is a steward of the shared conditions that enable human development. It creates the structural environment in which families, schools, workplaces, and civic organizations either struggle or thrive. It is frequently the largest employer and holds primary responsibility for addressing public safety, transportation infrastructure, and disaster relief.

Government culture—like any culture—is expressed through leadership behavior, public communication, institutional norms, accountability systems, and service delivery practices. When aligned with flourishing values, it strengthens public trust and societal resilience. This chapter examines how government can embody those values; what conditions broader society must create to support thriving governance; how flourishing in government can be meaningfully assessed; and how a flourishing societal culture helps government achieve its own deepest purposes.

The argument of this chapter rests on a central claim: the need for government intervention is substantially reduced when other institutions are functioning well. When families are stable, workplaces are fair, schools are strong, and civic organizations are vital, people have the support, accountability, and opportunity they need without heavy reliance on the state. Government, in this vision, is not the primary engine of flourishing—it is the enabling architecture and the protective backstop. It creates the conditions in which other institutions can do their best work, and it catches what they cannot hold when they fall short.

This is a demanding standard. It means that when a family fractures, when a workplace exploits, when a community loses its civic life, or when an individual makes a serious mistake, the government must be genuinely capable of providing adequate support and meaningful opportunity for recovery. A flourishing society does not abandon people at the moments when other institutions have failed them. It maintains the capacity—through social insurance, public services, legal protection, and community investment—to offer a path back toward participation and dignity. The quality of a society's safety net is not determined solely by its generosity. It is a measure of its confidence that people deserve the chance to recover, contribute, and flourish again.

A word of honesty is warranted here. Government can itself become a source of institutional dysfunction rather than a remedy for it. Poorly designed regulations can suppress entrepreneurship and community initiatives that are essential to flourishing. Captured agencies can serve narrow interests rather than the public good. Laws written with good intentions can produce harmful consequences. A flourishing government is not simply a larger or more active one—it is a wise one: clear about what it should do, humble about what it cannot, and continuously attentive to the effects of its own actions on the institutions it is meant to support.

I. Embodying Flourishing Values in Government

1. Productive Work

The government plays a central role in enabling productive work across society. It establishes infrastructure, protects property rights, supports fair markets, and invests in workforce development.

A flourishing government:

- promotes stable economic conditions,
- invests in transportation, digital, and civic infrastructure,
- ensures fair labor protections,
- encourages entrepreneurship and innovation, and
- aligns fiscal policy with long-term productivity.

Internally, government agencies must model productive work cultures—clear mission alignment, efficient processes, professional standards, and accountability.

When government functions effectively, it creates conditions in which individuals and businesses can contribute meaningfully to the common good.

2. Health

The government safeguards public health and safety through regulation, emergency response, environmental protection, and health care systems.

A flourishing government:

- ensures access to affordable health care,
- invests in preventive care and mental health,
- protects clean air, clean water, and safe communities, and
- coordinates crisis response with transparency.

Public health policy has profound cultural implications. It affects stress levels, life expectancy, and overall societal resilience.

Internally, thriving government agencies also prioritize employee well-being, reducing burnout and promoting sustainable public service careers.

3. Joy

Joy may seem distant from public policy, yet government decisions shape the conditions in which joy can flourish.

A flourishing government:

- protects public parks, cultural institutions, and the arts,
- invests in recreation and community spaces,
- encourages festivals, civic celebrations, and cultural expression,
- reduces unnecessary bureaucratic friction in daily life.

Public spaces that invite gathering and celebration strengthen social cohesion. When citizens experience beauty, culture, and shared events, civic pride increases. This is not merely aesthetic. Access to parks, arts, and community celebrations has measurable effects on mental health, loneliness, and the sense of belonging that sustains civic participation. Government investment in shared spaces and cultural life is an investment in the social fabric itself.

4. Kindness

Kindness in government is demonstrated through fairness, transparency, and respectful treatment of citizens.

Flourishing government cultures:

- deliver services with dignity and clarity,
- reduce unnecessary administrative burdens,
- communicate honestly and respectfully,
- protect minority rights while upholding democratic processes.

Kindness is not a weakness. It is a commitment to treating citizens as partners rather than obstacles, strengthening legitimacy and trust.

5. Learning

Effective governance requires adaptability. A flourishing government embraces continuous learning.

This includes:

- Evidence-based policymaking,
- Transparent data collection and evaluation,
- Cross-agency collaboration,
- Willingness to revise policies based on outcomes.

Learning-oriented governments avoid rigidity. They experiment thoughtfully and refine their practices over time.

6. Connection

The government fosters connection through civic participation, inclusive dialogue, and democratic processes.

A flourishing government:

- encourages citizen engagement,
- protects voting access and fair representation,
- facilitates public forums and deliberation,
- supports local governance and community leadership.

Connection in governance strengthens shared identity and social trust. When citizens feel heard and represented, civic engagement rises. Among the most foundational commitments a government makes to connection is protecting the integrity of democratic participation itself. Voting access and fair representation are not peripheral procedural matters—they are the mechanisms by which citizens exercise their voice in the institutions that govern their lives. A flourishing government works to ensure that participation in democratic processes is genuinely available: that registration is accessible, that polling is practical, that districts are drawn to represent communities rather than entrench incumbents, and that the rules governing elections are designed to produce legitimate outcomes that citizens across the political spectrum can accept as fair. Where these foundations erode, the connection between government and governed deteriorates—and with it, the social trust on which everything else in this chapter depends.

II. How Society Can Support Thriving Government Cultures

Government culture does not evolve in isolation. Citizen expectations, media narratives, economic pressures, and political norms shape it.

If society seeks flourishing governance, it must cultivate the conditions that support it.

1. Civic Education

Informed citizens are essential to healthy governance. Education systems that teach democratic processes, critical thinking, and respectful dialogue enhance government effectiveness.

2. Constructive Political Discourse

Polarization and hostility erode institutional trust. Cultural norms that value civil debate and evidence-based arguments foster healthier public institutions.

3. Ethical Leadership Development

Investing in leadership training for public servants strengthens professionalism and integrity across agencies.

4. Responsible Media Ecosystems

Accurate, balanced journalism supports transparency and accountability while reducing misinformation that can undermine trust. This is among the most consequential structural challenges of contemporary governance. Governments depend on a shared factual foundation—an information environment in which citizens and officials can debate policy in good faith, evaluate evidence together, and hold institutions accountable based on what is actually happening. When that foundation is degraded by deliberate disinformation, by economic pressures that reward outrage over accuracy, or by the fragmentation of media into ideologically isolated ecosystems, governance becomes dramatically harder. Governments cannot unilaterally create a trustworthy information environment—that responsibility is shared among media organizations, technology platforms, civic institutions, and individuals. But a flourishing society treats its information infrastructure as a public good worthy of protection and investment, understanding that the capacity for honest public deliberation is the precondition for everything else democratic governance aspires to achieve.

5. Citizen Engagement

Participation in voting, public meetings, and community dialogue reinforces accountability. Governments thrive when citizens remain engaged rather than disengaged or cynical.

6. Long-Term Policy Orientation

Short election cycles can encourage short-term thinking. Cultural expectations that prioritize long-term planning and sustainability strengthen public institutions. This is among the deepest structural tensions in democratic governance. The investments most important for long-term flourishing—in infrastructure, education, public health, environmental protection, and scientific research—often produce their most visible returns decades after the leaders who made them have left office. The harms most important to prevent—fiscal imbalances, ecological degradation, deteriorating public institutions—accumulate gradually, making them easy to defer and politically costly to address. A flourishing society cultivates the civic maturity to demand long-term thinking from its leaders: to reward politicians who make difficult decisions for future benefit rather than only those who deliver immediate gratification, and to hold governments accountable not only for what they accomplished in the last term but for the condition of the institutions they will leave behind.

Thriving government cultures require both capable institutions and responsible civic partnerships.

III. Assessing Flourishing in Government

Intentional governance requires intentional evaluation. A flourishing assessment framework for government could include:

A. Shared Values Alignment

- Clarity of mission across agencies
- Alignment between policy goals and public values
- Transparency in decision-making processes

B. Public Trust and Legitimacy

- Citizen trust metrics
- Perceived fairness and integrity
- Participation rates in elections and civic forums

C. Service Effectiveness

- Efficiency of service delivery
- Accessibility and clarity of public programs
- Response time to citizen inquiries

D. Health and Sustainability

- Public health indicators
- Environmental quality measures
- Fiscal sustainability metrics
- Employee retention and burnout within agencies

E. Learning and Adaptation

- Use of evidence in policymaking
- Policy evaluation systems
- Responsiveness to feedback
- Innovation in service design

F. Relational Strength

- Collaboration across agencies
- Partnerships with civic and community organizations
- Inclusion of diverse perspectives in policymaking

Assessment tools may include public surveys, performance dashboards, independent audits, and structured policy reviews. The aim is continuous alignment with flourishing values rather than static compliance.

IV. How a Flourishing Societal Culture Supports Government

The relationship between government and society runs in both directions. Government shapes the conditions in which people and institutions flourish or struggle. But a flourishing societal culture also makes good governance more achievable—providing the civic foundation without which even well-designed institutions falter.

What does the government most deeply seek to achieve? Beyond administering services and enforcing laws, government aspires to something more fundamental: creating and maintaining the conditions in which everyone has a genuine opportunity to live well. It seeks a society stable enough to plan ahead, fair enough that people trust its rules, and capable enough to respond when individuals and communities are overwhelmed. A flourishing societal culture actively advances each of these goals in ways that government cannot accomplish alone.

When families are strong, workplaces are fair, schools are effective, and civic organizations are active, the demand on government is genuinely reduced. People in well-functioning communities resolve more conflicts before they reach legal systems. They support each other through setbacks before they require public assistance. They build the social trust that makes public institutions feel legitimate rather than alien. A flourishing culture is not a substitute for capable government—it is the environment in which government can operate at its best, focusing its resources on problems that genuinely require collective action rather than compensating for the collapse of other forms of social support.

A flourishing culture also sustains the civic virtues on which democratic governance depends. When citizens approach political disagreement with the expectation of good faith rather than contempt, when they hold their own side accountable rather than only the opposition, when they understand that public institutions belong to everyone and must be defended as such, government becomes dramatically more capable. These are not naïve hopes. They are descriptions of what democratic societies have achieved in their better moments—and what they must actively cultivate to sustain.

Perhaps most importantly, a flourishing societal culture extends generous expectations to those who have stumbled. When society broadly believes that people deserve the opportunity to recover from failure—whether that failure was personal, economic, or institutional—it is far easier for government to design and sustain the programs that make recovery possible. Conversely, when a culture treats those in need of support as moral failures rather than as people in difficult circumstances, the political will to maintain an adequate safety net erodes. The quality of the government's protective capacity ultimately reflects the quality of the cultural values that surround it.

Government as Steward of Collective Conditions

The government shapes the structural context within which other institutions operate. It can either amplify stress, fragmentation, and inequity—or create stability, opportunity, and trust.

When the government embraces productive work, health, joy, kindness, learning, and connection, it strengthens the foundations of societal flourishing. It provides the guardrails and infrastructure that allow communities, organizations, and individuals to thrive.

A flourishing society does not require perfect governance. It requires committed stewardship—institutions that evolve, learn, and serve with integrity. When government culture aligns with human development and shared purpose, public institutions become not only policy instruments but also pillars of flourishing. But the stakes of getting this right are unlike those of any other chapter in this book. Government is not one institution among equals. It is the institution that sets the structural conditions within which all other institutions operate. What it does with its extraordinary authority either makes large-scale flourishing possible—or forecloses it. When government protects the rule of law, invests in shared infrastructure, maintains genuine opportunity for those who have fallen, and steps back to let families, communities, workplaces, and civic life do what they do best, it becomes the invisible architecture of a society that flourishes. When it fails in these responsibilities—through neglect, capture, short-termism, or the erosion of democratic norms—the damage ripples through every other institution described in this book. A flourishing society, therefore, demands serious, sustained, and honest engagement with the quality of its governance—not as a partisan project but as a shared commitment to the conditions on which everything else depends.

PART III
BUILDING A FLOURISHING SOCIETY TOGETHER

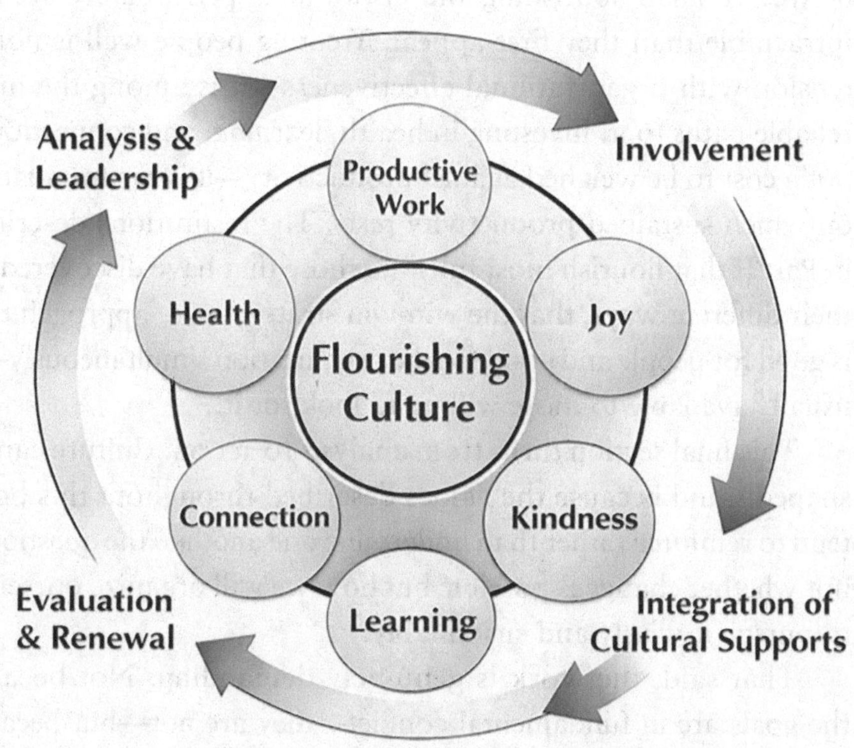

THE FIRST SECTION of this book examined the elements of culture—the values, norms, peer relationships, leadership patterns, social climate, and cultural touchpoints that quietly shape daily life. The second section explored how these dynamics operate across major social institutions, including family, education, government, healthcare, finance, and technology. Together, those chapters advanced one central claim: flourishing is not accidental. It is the predictable result of cultural conditions that consistently reinforce productive work, health, joy, kindness, learning, and connection. Those chapters also advanced a second, quieter claim: that the apparent trade-offs between human flourishing and institutional performance are less intractable than they first appear. Treating people well is not in tension with organizational effectiveness—it is among the most reliable paths to it. Investing in health, learning, and connection is not a cost to be weighed against productivity—it is the foundation on which sustained productivity rests. The institutions described in Part II that flourish most fully are those that have discovered, in their different ways, that the win-win strategy—the approach that is good for people and good for the organization simultaneously—is usually available to those willing to look for it.

This final section turns from analysis to action. Culture can be shaped—and because the values described throughout this book tend to reinforce rather than undermine one another, the question is not whether change is possible but how we will organize ourselves to pursue it wisely and sustainably.

That said, the work is genuinely demanding. Not because the goals are in fundamental conflict—they are not—but because translating good values into lasting cultural change requires skill, patience, coordination, and the willingness to stay the course when progress demands creativity, cooperation, and follow-through.

Win-win strategies do not implement themselves. They require leaders who can see the larger opportunity, peers willing to model new norms, and institutions ready to align their incentive structures with their stated values. This section is a practical guide to doing that work well.

Before turning to the framework for pursuing that work, Chapter 16 offers something equally important: evidence that it is worth pursuing. Across six cases—a prison, a factory floor, a national culture, a technology company, a community health initiative, and a worker cooperative—that chapter documents what flourishing cultures look like when built intentionally. These are not utopias. Each has faced real pressures and imperfections. But together, they demonstrate that aligning values, norms, leadership, and structure around human dignity produces outcomes that neither purely market-driven nor purely compliance-driven approaches can match. They are evidence, not prescription—a reminder that the invitation extended in the pages that follow is grounded in past achievements.

Start Where You Stand

Large-scale societal change can feel abstract or overwhelming. Yet culture does not exist only at the national or global level. It also lives in smaller, tangible settings—families, workplaces, professional associations, faith communities, classrooms, civic groups, and neighborhoods. These are the environments we know intimately. They are the places where we already have relationships, credibility, and influence.

Rather than waiting for sweeping reforms imposed from above, this section recommends starting with the groups and environments you know best. A teacher can help cultivate a flourishing classroom culture. A manager can strengthen a team's norms of kindness and learning. A healthcare leader can reinforce dignity and connection in patient care. A civic volunteer can support constructive dialogue and shared purpose.

Systemic transformation begins locally, relationally, and concretely. The most striking illustration of this in the chapters that follow is also the most extreme: Nelson Mandela and his fellow prisoners on Robben Island, who built what they came to call a university—a culture of learning, mutual respect, and long-term purpose—inside one of the most constrained environments imaginable. They had no institutional resources, no authority over their conditions, and no guarantee that their work would matter. What they had was intention and a shared commitment to the values that would outlast their imprisonment. If a flourishing culture can be built there, it can be built anywhere.

When multiple subcultures align around flourishing values, the broader culture gradually shifts. Change accumulates.

Work from a Sound Information Base

Culture change is complex. It involves interdependent systems of expectations, incentives, leadership signals, and peer reinforcement—people immersed in a culture become acculturated. The subtle influences become less visible and may be overlooked. Strengths and opportunities must be assessed first. As a result, analysis frequently requires careful consideration of how the cultural web of values, norms, leadership support, peer support, touchpoints, and social climate shape attitudes and behavior. A sound information base often requires a multi-method strategy including observation, interviews, surveys, and field experiments. It is often necessary to dispel myths and misunderstandings before meaningful change can be planned.

A Systematic, Four-Phase Approach

Attempting to change everything at once often leads to burnout or fragmentation. The sequence matters as much as the steps. Organizations that move too quickly to implementation—before leadership is aligned or people understand what is being asked of them—often generate resistance that hardens into cynicism. Those who skip the reflective phase miss the feedback loops that allow them to correct course.

The four-phase approach described here is designed to prevent these common failures by ensuring that each stage lays the foundation the next requires.

For that reason, this section presents a structured four-phase approach to culture change—an approach that organizes complex transformation into manageable, coherent stages. Although the phases will be described in detail in the chapters that follow, the basic rhythm is:

1. **Analysis, Objective Setting, and Leadership Support** – Identify which flourishing values are most relevant in your setting and evaluate current cultural strengths and gaps. Develop leaders' capacity to support culture change.
2. **Involve People** – Cultural members need to understand what is being done, why it is important, and how they can support the effort.
3. **Implement and Support** – Align touchpoints, develop individual skills, and mobilize peer and leadership support.
4. **Reflect and Refine** – Measure progress, learn from setbacks, and make iterative adjustments.

By organizing change into phases, complexity becomes manageable. Energy is focused where it is most needed. Effort becomes cumulative rather than chaotic. Progress becomes measurable rather than aspirational.

Cooperation, not Isolation

No single individual can create a flourishing society alone. Culture is relational; it is constructed and sustained collectively. Therefore, this section emphasizes the importance of joining with others—within your organization, across professions, and across institutions.

Partnership multiplies impact and increases resilience. When multiple leaders and peer groups reinforce the same values, new norms stabilize more quickly. Shared language develops. Success stories spread. Confidence grows. And flourishing, it turns out, is contagious: a manager who builds a thriving team attracts people who carry those norms into future roles; a school known for its culture of learning raises the expectations of every institution it touches. Visible success lowers the perceived risk of imitation and raises the perceived cost of the status quo. The spread is not automatic but predictable.

This is the ultimate aim of the work described in Part III: not a society that requires exceptional people to behave exceptionally but one whose ordinary structures and expectations make flourishing the path of least resistance. The goal is a culture that does the work, so that individuals do not have to carry it alone. Chapter 16 offers evidence that this threshold is real—and reachable.

The Invitation

This final section invites a shift from reflection to shared stewardship—the ongoing, cooperative work of tending the cultural environments we inhabit and influence. Each of us participates in multiple subcultures. Each of us shapes expectations, signals values, and reinforces norms—sometimes subtly, sometimes visibly. That participation is not incidental to culture change. It is culture change.

By becoming more intentional about how we contribute to these environments, we help shape the broader society.

The work is cooperative. It is systematic. It is incremental. And it is possible.

The next chapter, Where to Begin, offers practical guidance for readers who are ready to take the first steps—helping you identify where your own influence is greatest, what conditions to assess, and how to enter a culture change effort with both clarity and humility.

A flourishing society will not be built by accident. It will be cultivated—one aligned environment at a time—until the values that support human dignity and collective well-being are woven into the fabric of everyday life.

Chapter 16
Examples of Flourishing Cultures in Action

Flourishing cultures are not theoretical. Across history and across sectors, groups have demonstrated that when shared values, norms, leadership, peer support, touchpoints, and social climate align around human dignity and growth, remarkable outcomes follow.

These examples are not perfect societies, nor are they timeless. They are instructive cases—illustrations of how intentional cultural design can strengthen productive work, health, joy, kindness, learning, and connection at a particular moment, in a particular context. Each example is in some sense date-stamped: the conditions that made it remarkable were shaped by specific leadership, historical circumstances, and surrounding pressures that have since shifted. New revelations and changing circumstances often undermine standout cultures, and some of the evidence supporting these cases has been partially revised. One or more of these examples likely would not qualify today as a flourishing culture in full operation. What they retain is instructive value—evidence of what becomes possible when the elements of culture align intentionally around human dignity, even if that alignment proved difficult to sustain.

1. Moral Courage and Cultural Resilience: Nelson Mandela and Robben Island

One of the most powerful examples of flourishing within severe constraint occurred inside Robben Island prison during apartheid. What makes this case so instructive is precisely what made it so unlikely: the prisoners had no resources, no institutional support, and no authority over their physical conditions. What they built—a culture of dignity, learning, and long-term purpose—they built entirely from intention and collective commitment.

Conditions were harsh. Prisoners endured physical labor, limited communication, and systemic dehumanization. Yet Mandela and his fellow prisoners intentionally cultivated a counter-culture within the prison walls.

Shared Values

They anchored themselves in dignity, learning, discipline, and long-term purpose.

Norms

They established norms of mutual respect and intellectual seriousness.

Peer Support

They formed study groups—sometimes referred to as a "university"—teaching law, politics, language, and history.

Leadership Support

Mandela modeled composure, respect toward guards, and commitment to reconciliation.

Touchpoints

Daily routines reinforced education, reflection, and collective identity.

Social Climate

Despite confinement, many prisoners described a sense of meaning and solidarity.

The lesson: even in highly constrained environments, aligned cultural elements can sustain human flourishing and strengthen long-term resilience. A note on the date-stamp: this culture was a product of its particular moment—shaped by Mandela's exceptional leadership and the moral clarity of a liberation struggle. Subsequent South African history has been more complicated, and many of the values cultivated on Robben Island have faced significant pressure in post-apartheid institutions. The lesson endures; the cultural conditions that produced it were always fragile and historically specific.

2. Industrial Renewal Through Human Dignity: Toyota and the Toyota Production System

The Toyota Production System (TPS) became globally influential not only for its efficiency but also for its cultural philosophy. At its core, TPS embodied a claim that most industrial organizations of its era rejected: that the people doing the work are also the people best positioned to improve it. The Andon cord—which allowed any worker to stop the production line to correct a defect—was not merely a quality tool. It was a structural expression of that belief, embedding dignity and problem-solving authority in the factory floor's physical environment.

Shared Values

Respect for people and continuous improvement (kaizen).

Norms

Workers are expected—and empowered—to identify problems.

Peer Support

Teams collaborate to solve operational challenges.

Leadership Support

Supervisors function as coaches rather than authoritarian overseers.

Touchpoints

The andon cord allows any worker to stop the production line to correct a defect—embedding quality and dignity into daily operations.

Social Climate

Psychological safety around problem identification reduces fear and encourages learning.

The result was improved productivity and quality—but also a model showing that productive work and human respect can reinforce one another. A note on the date-stamp: TPS was developed under specific cultural and competitive conditions in postwar Japan, and its transplantation to other national contexts has produced uneven results. Toyota itself has faced subsequent quality and safety controversies—including high-profile recalls—that raised questions about whether its cultural philosophy had been adequately maintained as the company scaled globally. The model's principles remain sound and widely applied; whether any particular implementation lives up to them is always a live question.

3. High Trust and Social Well-Being: Denmark

Denmark frequently ranks highly in measures of trust, life satisfaction, and social cohesion—and has done so consistently enough across decades that it represents something more durable than a momentary peak. What is most instructive about Denmark is not any single policy but the degree to which multiple systems—welfare, governance, education, civic participation—have been aligned over time around a shared set of values.

Shared Values
Strong social safety nets, work-life balance, and egalitarianism.

Norms
Modesty, civic participation, and cooperative problem-solving.

Peer Support
Community associations and local participation are common practices.

Leadership Support
Transparent governance and relatively low corruption strengthen institutional trust.

Touchpoints
Policies reinforce access to health care, parental leave, and education.

Social Climate
High interpersonal trust reduces chronic stress and fosters a sense of belonging.

While no nation is without challenges, Denmark shows how policy, norms, and social climate can align to support population-level flourishing. A note on generalizability and the date-stamp: Denmark's achievements reflect conditions—a small, historically homogeneous population, strong institutional inheritance, and decades of political consensus—that are not easily transplanted.

Researchers continue to debate how much of Denmark's well-being is attributable to intentional cultural design versus structural advantages. More recently, Denmark has faced rising political polarization, immigration-related tensions, and pressure on the welfare state from global economic forces. These challenges do not erase the lesson; they underscore that even the most durably flourishing cultures require active maintenance.

4. Psychological Safety and Learning: Google and Project Aristotle

Google's internal study, Project Aristotle, examined the factors that made teams effective. It was a landmark piece of organizational research, both for its rigor and for what it found: that team composition, skill level, and individual talent mattered less than the quality of the team's social environment—and, most of all, whether members felt safe taking interpersonal risks.

The most important factor was psychological safety.

Shared Values

Open communication and experimentation.

Norms

Admitting mistakes without humiliation.

Peer Support

Active listening and inclusive conversation patterns.

Leadership Support

Managers are trained to encourage input from all members.

Touchpoints

Performance systems increasingly recognize collaborative behavior.

Social Climate

Teams with psychological safety exhibited higher levels of innovation and engagement.

The broader lesson: learning cultures require safety. Without it, knowledge is withheld. A note on the date-stamp: Project Aristotle captured conditions at a particular period in Google's development. Google has since faced well-publicized internal conflicts over labor practices, content moderation decisions, and employee dissent—raising serious questions about whether the psychological safety the research described was ever uniformly distributed or has been maintained. The findings about what makes teams effective remain well supported across research settings; Google, as an ongoing institution, is a separate and more contested story.

5. Community Health Transformation: Blue Zones Project

Inspired by research on longevity regions, the Blue Zones Project partners with cities to shift environmental and cultural conditions. What makes this case methodologically distinctive—and instructive—is its explicit attempt to move the unit of change from the individual to the community: rather than asking people to adopt healthier behaviors through willpower, it redesigns the surrounding environment to make healthier behaviors the default.

Shared Values

Health, connection, and purpose.

Norms

Walking meetings, plant-forward diets, and social engagement.

Peer Support

Community groups commit to shared lifestyle practices.

Leadership Support

Municipal leaders endorse environmental redesign.

Touchpoints

Restaurant labeling, school programming, and urban planning changes.

Social Climate

Health becomes socially reinforced rather than an individual burden.

Communities that have adopted these shifts have reported improvements in well-being indicators and collective engagement. A note on the date-stamp and evidence: this is the case most directly affected by subsequent scrutiny. The original longevity research underlying the Blue Zones concept has faced significant methodological criticism—including questions about data quality, age verification, and the role of poverty (which reduces longevity-extending medical interventions) in inflating apparent lifespan statistics. The applied Blue Zones Project, which draws on this research, has reported improvements in community well-being that are harder to verify independently. The underlying principle—that environmental and social design shapes health behavior at scale—remains well supported. The specific evidentiary claims deserve to be held with appropriate caution.

6. Cooperative Economics and Shared Ownership: Mondragon Corporation

Founded in Spain's Basque region, Mondragon is a federation of worker cooperatives that began in 1956 under the guidance of a Catholic priest, José María Arizmendiarrieta, who believed that economic structure could itself be a vehicle for human dignity. What Mondragon represents is a sustained, large-scale demonstration that democratic ownership and competitive performance are not mutually exclusive—that fairness can be built into how an organization functions rather than bolted on as an afterthought.

Shared Values

Democratic participation, solidarity, and shared prosperity.

Norms

Open financial transparency and participatory governance.

Peer Support

Workers are co-owners with shared stakes.

Leadership Support

Leaders are elected and accountable.

Touchpoints

Compensation ratios limit income disparities within cooperatives.

Social Climate

High levels of belonging and shared purpose.

Mondragon demonstrates how economic structure itself can become a cultural touchpoint that reinforces connection and fairness. A note on the date-stamp: Mondragon has faced significant pressures of its own. The collapse of Fagor, one of its largest cooperatives, in 2013—following the 2008 financial crisis—was a painful demonstration that cooperative ownership does not insulate an organization from global economic forces. Some critics have also noted that Mondragon's international subsidiaries employ non-owner workers on conventional terms, raising questions about whether its ownership values have been meaningfully extended or partially diluted as the federation has grown. The core model remains operational and instructive; the complications are worth knowing about.

Cross-Case Insights: What Flourishing Cultures Share

Across these diverse settings—prison resistance movements, manufacturing systems, national cultures, technology companies, public health initiatives, and worker cooperatives—common themes emerge:

1. Alignment Across Elements

Flourishing cultures do not rely on a single inspiring leader or a single policy. Values, norms, leadership behavior, touchpoints, peer support, and climate align.

2. Reinforcement Over Rhetoric

Statements alone do not create culture. Systems reinforce what is real.

3. Learning Orientation

Each example emphasizes reflection, adaptation, and shared inquiry.

4. Human Dignity as Operational Principle

Whether in a factory or a prison yard, flourishing begins with the belief that people deserve respect and growth.

5. Long-Term Orientation

Short-term efficiency without long-term well-being rarely leads to durable flourishing.

Caution and Realism

These examples are not utopias, nor are they permanent achievements. Each has faced internal conflicts, leadership challenges, economic pressures, and cultural tensions—and some have been significantly altered or diminished by them. The date-stamp notes appended to each case are not incidental caveats. They are part of the lesson.

Flourishing cultures are dynamic and historically situated. The conditions that sustain them—aligned leadership, supportive norms, reinforcing structures, and a surrounding environment that does not actively undermine them—are never guaranteed to persist. Cultures that flourished in one era have been eroded by new competitive pressures, leadership succession failures, ideological shifts, or simply the difficulty of maintaining alignment across scale and time. This is not a reason for pessimism; it is a reason for ongoing attention.

What distinguishes these cases is not that they solved the problem permanently but that they solved it meaningfully—and that they did so intentionally. The evidence of their achievement survives even when the achievement itself does not.

Implications

The purpose of these examples is not imitation but orientation. None of them is a template. Each arose in a specific context, under specific conditions, and with specific constraints that limit direct replication. What they offer instead is a set of confirmed possibilities: that dignity can be fostered even in the most constrained environments; that productive work and genuine well-being can reinforce rather than undercut each other; that policy and cultural norms shape social climate at scale; that structural design—how ownership, compensation, decision-making, and accountability are arranged—powerfully influences trust; that leadership modeling shapes what people around it believe is normal; and that the touchpoints and reinforcement structures an organization builds ultimately determine whether its stated values take root or wither. These are not aspirational claims. They are documented outcomes from real settings. The examples are date-stamped; the lessons are not.

Flourishing cultures are built—not by accident but by intention.

The question is not whether flourishing cultures exist.

The question is whether we are willing to design them.

Chapter 17

Deciding Where to Begin

Strategic Entry Points for Culture Change

One of the most consequential decisions in any culture change effort is deceptively simple: Where do we begin? The question sounds like a practical matter of sequencing, but it is really a strategic one. The answer shapes whether early effort builds momentum or dissipates into discouragement, whether success stories spread or remain isolated, and whether the initiative earns enough credibility to grow.

Beginning everywhere is impossible. Beginning nowhere is common. Beginning strategically is essential.

Flourishing spreads through social systems, but it does not spread evenly. Research on the diffusion of innovations—particularly the work of Everett Rogers, who studied how new ideas and practices spread across communities and organizations—shows that change accelerates when it begins with credible early adopters in environments that are receptive, visible, and well connected to the broader system. Early adopters are people and groups who take up a new practice before most others do, and whose credibility makes the practice visible and legible to those observing from a distance. Their success answers the question that most potential adopters are quietly asking: Does this actually work for people like us?

But receptivity is not only a matter of structural position or leadership alignment. It is also emotional and relational. The social climate of a group—the level of trust, shared purpose, and realistic hope among its members—plays a decisive role in whether change can take root at all. Even well-designed initiatives stall in climates marked by distrust, fragmentation, or entrenched cynicism. Conversely, in environments characterized by cohesion and honest optimism, even modest efforts can grow quickly into something durable.

This chapter offers a framework for making that choice wisely. It begins with the social climate, which is the most important factor to assess before selecting a starting point. It then examines the other dimensions of readiness and leverage that distinguish strong entry points and describes four strategic approaches to entering a change effort. It closes with a practical diagnostic tool—the Social Climate Assessment—that you can use to evaluate any candidate setting before committing resources and attention to it.

Once you have identified where to begin, the four-phase culture change model described in the chapters that follow provides the framework for how to proceed. This chapter answers the prior question.

I. The Role of Social Climate

Before selecting a starting point—whether a household, peer group, workplace unit, civic organization, or neighborhood—

assess the strength of the social climate. Social climate is not the same as morale or satisfaction, though those are related. It refers specifically to the degree to which a group has the relational and motivational foundations that enable intentional change: a sense of belonging among members, a shared understanding of why their work matters, and a realistic belief that improvement is achievable.

These three elements—sense of community, shared vision, and positive outlook—are not merely nice-to-haves. They are the medium through which cultural change travels. Without a sense of belonging, people do not trust the intentions behind new initiatives. Without a shared vision, efforts feel arbitrary rather than meaningful. Without realistic hope, even good early results fail to generate momentum because members interpret them as anomalies rather than evidence of what is possible.

A strong social climate does not mean a conflict-free or perfectly harmonious environment. It means that three conditions are sufficiently present to support honest dialogue and collaborative effort.

1. Sense of Community

Members feel they belong and that their presence matters. Relationships are generally respectful, even across disagreements. Collaboration is more common than internal competition. People feel safe enough to speak honestly, including about what is not working.

2. Shared Vision

There is sufficient clarity of purpose for members to understand why their work or relationships matter. Goals are broadly aligned, and people's efforts feel connected to something meaningful rather than arbitrary or externally imposed.

3. Positive (Realistic) Outlook

Members believe that improvement is possible—not guaranteed but genuinely available to people like them in settings like this one. Challenges are framed as problems to be addressed rather than evidence of permanent dysfunction. There is some track record of past success to point to. Cynicism, while perhaps present, does not dominate.

Together, these three elements create the conditions that diffusion theory identifies as essential: trust in the channels of communication, credibility in those advocating change, and sufficient common ground to enable coordinated action. When the social climate is weak, change efforts must either begin elsewhere or invest in climate repair before launching. Flourishing cannot be imposed on a fractured social field. It must grow in relationally viable soil.

II. Choosing the Right Entry Point

Flourishing can begin in any subculture—a household, a friendship circle, a department, a professional team, a neighborhood association, a civic or faith community, or a mission-driven organization. The key is not scale. A small, well-aligned team can initiate more durable change than a large, fractured department. The key is readiness and leverage: readiness to reflect and act, and leverage to make success visible and influence adjacent environments.

When evaluating a candidate entry point, seven factors deserve assessment. Not all carry equal weight in every situation, but each can be the decisive variable in whether an effort succeeds.

1. Readiness

Is there awareness within the group that something needs to change, or that a genuine opportunity exists? Readiness does not require urgency or crisis—in fact, crisis often degrades the reflective capacity needed for good culture work. But it does require some openness to honest examination of current conditions and some appetite for doing things differently.

2. Social Climate Strength

As described in Section I, this is the most important structural condition. A group with strong climate and modest leadership is often more productive than a group with weak climate and excellent leadership, because climate determines whether the relational infrastructure for change is in place.

3. Leadership Commitment

Are the formal and informal leaders of this group willing to model the changes being sought? Leaders who endorse change rhetorically but do not visibly alter their own behavior create a credibility gap that is very difficult to close. The question is not whether leaders are enthusiastic—it is whether they are willing to go first.

4. Trust Levels

Is there sufficient psychological safety for honest dialogue? Culture change requires people to name what is not working, experiment with unfamiliar practices, and sometimes acknowledge failure. These actions all require trust. Groups with low trust levels can build them—but that work should precede, not accompany, a full change initiative.

5. Visibility

Will success in this group be noticed by others in the broader system? Visibility is what converts a local win into a catalyst for wider change. A team that quietly and in isolation transforms its culture may do important work, but it does not accelerate diffusion. Groups that are admired, envied, or regularly observed by adjacent groups have higher leverage for the same amount of effort.

6. *Feasibility*

Is the scope manageable, and can measurable progress be demonstrated within a reasonable timeframe—typically 6 to 12 months? Efforts that take years to show any visible result lose momentum and lose the narrative. Early wins are not just motivating; they are the evidence that makes the case to skeptical observers that the approach is credible.

7. *Structural Reinforcement Potential*

Can this group influence the routines, recognition systems, or policies that shape daily behavior? Groups that control meaningful cultural touchpoints—how people are recognized, how meetings are run, what gets celebrated, how decisions are made—can embed new norms into structure rather than relying on individual willpower and memory. Structural reinforcement is what makes change durable rather than episodic.

These seven factors do not carry equal weight in every situation, and they interact with one another. A group with a moderately strong climate but exceptional potential for structural reinforcement and visibility might be a stronger starting point than a group with a strong climate and low visibility. The framework is a judgment aid, not a formula. What it consistently points toward is this: the strongest entry points combine a moderate-to-high social climate with visibility and the potential for structural reinforcement.

These factors play out differently across scales. A household or tight peer group tends to have naturally high trust and cohesion but low visibility and limited structural leverage. A department or civic organization has more structural power but often a more fractured climate. A neighborhood association may have visibility within a community but limited authority over cultural touchpoints. Knowing the trade-offs of different entry scales helps avoid either starting too small (insufficient reach) or too large (insufficient cohesion).

III. Strategic Entry Approaches

Given the factors above, four strategic patterns are especially common and effective. Each reflects a different starting condition and a distinct theory of how change spreads.

The Micro-Culture Strategy

Begin in a small relational unit—a family, a peer circle, a tight team—where high cohesion allows rapid experimentation. The micro-culture strategy works because close relationships reduce the social risk of trying new behaviors and provide immediate feedback on what is and is not working. The limitation is visibility: success in a micro-culture may not be noticed by the broader system unless it is deliberately surfaced and shared.

The Leadership Anchor Strategy

Begin with leaders who visibly model the values and behaviors associated with flourishing. Because structural signals—what leaders do, tolerate, and celebrate—shape the behavior of everyone in the system, leadership-anchored change can reach a broad population relatively quickly. The risk is that a perceived "top-down" change may generate compliance without genuine adoption, particularly if leaders' behavior is seen as performative rather than authentic.

This strategy is strongest when leaders are genuinely committed and when peer reinforcement is built alongside the leadership signal.

The Pilot Strategy

Launch in one well-chosen unit with the explicit goal of demonstrating measurable results before scaling. The pilot strategy manages risk and generates evidence. It is particularly valuable in organizations where skepticism is high, because visible results in a credible unit can shift the burden of proof. Instead of advocates having to prove the approach will work, skeptics now have to explain why the pilot results do not apply to them. The pilot must be chosen carefully: a unit that is unusually advantaged will produce results that others dismiss as non-generalizable.

The Hybrid Strategy

Combine leadership endorsement with genuine grassroots participation. This pattern, when executed well, tends to produce the most durable diffusion of the four—because it creates simultaneous reinforcement from above (structural signals, resources, permission) and from below (peer modeling, authentic adoption, local ownership). It is also the most complex to coordinate. The risk is that top-down and bottom-up efforts operate at cross-purposes, with leaders signaling one set of priorities and informal peer culture signaling another. When the two are aligned, diffusion is rapid and resilient.

IV. When Social Climate is Weak

Sometimes the setting that most needs culture change is also the one least ready to receive it. High-stakes environments—a struggling school, a burned-out team, a divided community organization—

often have the weakest social climates and therefore the lowest readiness for the kind of reflective, collaborative work that culture change requires. This is not a reason to abandon them. It is a reason to be honest about sequencing.

If a strategically important setting has a weak social climate, two paths are available. The first is to begin elsewhere—to build credibility and a visible track record in a more receptive environment, and then use that evidence to create the conditions for eventual engagement in the harder setting. The second is to invest in climate repair before launching a full culture change effort. This means building relational trust through low-stakes collaboration, clarifying shared purpose through honest conversation about what members actually value and want, generating small collaborative wins that demonstrate the group can succeed together, and increasing transparency about decisions and their rationale.

Neither path is fast, and neither guarantees success. But attempting to impose a flourishing initiative on a fractured social field—without attending to the relational and motivational conditions that make change possible—is almost always counterproductive. It breeds cynicism about change efforts in general, making future attempts harder. The patience required to repair the social climate before launching is not a detour; it is the most direct route available.

Social Climate Assessment

The following diagnostic is designed to be used before launching a culture change initiative. Invite members of the candidate group to rate each statement independently on a five-point scale. Aggregate the responses to get an inside picture of the group's social climate, which is often more accurate than an outside assessment and always more credible to the members themselves.

Rating scale: 1 = Strongly Disagree 2 = Disagree
3 = Neutral 4 = Agree 5 = Strongly Agree

A. Sense of Community

1. We care for one another in times of need.
2. We stay current on one another's activities and interests.
3. We have really gotten to know one another.
4. We trust one another.
5. We feel comfortable saying what's on our minds.
6. We look forward to a future together.
7. We feel a strong sense of belonging.

Community Subtotal (add scores): ______ /7

B. Shared Vision

1. We share common values.
2. We listen to each other.
3. We make decisions in inclusive and respectful ways.
4. We cooperate.
5. We have clear and consistent goals.
6. We share responsibility for making things work.
7. We give one another the freedom to do things in our own way.

Vision Subtotal (add scores): ______ /7

C. Positive Outlook

1. We maintain high standards.
2. We have a high level of team spirit.
3. We resolve conflicts in positive ways.

4. We celebrate achievements.
5. We have a can-do attitude.
6. We are proud of our group.
7. Challenges are discussed constructively.
8. We have experienced successful changes before.
9. Cynicism does not dominate conversations.

Outlook Subtotal (add scores): ______ /9
Total Social Climate Score: ______ /23

Interpreting Results

- **4–5 (Strong Climate):** High readiness. This group is an excellent candidate for early adoption. Proceed to the entry strategy that best fits your context.
- **3-4 (Moderate Climate):** Viable starting point. Consider modest climate-strengthening work—a few shared wins, increased transparency, or a structured conversation about purpose—before full launch.
- **2-3 (Fragile Climate):** Proceed cautiously. Begin with explicit trust-building and shared-vision conversations before attempting broader culture change. Be prepared for this work to take time.
- **Below 2 (Weak Climate):** Either start elsewhere and return to this setting once you have a track record, or invest substantially in climate repair before proceeding.

Subscale scores are also informative. A group that scores well on community and vision but poorly on outlook may need a different intervention than one that scores well on outlook but poorly on trust. Each subscale points to a specific kind of preparatory work.

Conclusion: Begin Where Growth is Possible

The question is not whether flourishing is desirable. It is where flourishing can first take root. That is a question of strategy, not ambition—and answering it well is one of the most important contributions you can make to the long-term success of a culture change effort.

Flourishing rarely begins everywhere at once. It begins where belonging exists, purpose is shared, hope is realistic, and leadership is open—and where early success is visible to others. From there, it expands. Visible results reshape expectations. Adjacent groups ask what changed and how. The credibility earned in one setting opens doors in the next.

The Social Climate Assessment in this chapter gives you a structured way to evaluate candidate settings before committing. But the framework itself is a discipline of attention: a reminder to look honestly at the relational conditions of a group before asking it to take on the additional work of intentional cultural change.

Once you have identified where to begin, the question shifts to how. The four-phase model in the chapters that follow—analysis and objective setting, involving people, implementing and supporting change, and reflecting and refining—provides the framework for the work ahead. This chapter has prepared you to enter that process in the right place, with clear eyes about what you are working with.

Chapter 18

Analyzing Flourishing in the Current Culture

IF WE WANT to cultivate a flourishing society, we must first learn to see clearly. Culture is powerful precisely because it is often invisible. It shapes what we reward, what we tolerate, what we expect, and what we quietly ignore. Without systematic analysis, we risk mistaking cultural side effects for personal shortcomings or isolated institutional failures—blaming individuals for patterns the system produces.

Most cultural analyses fail for a predictable reason: they examine cultural elements in isolation. An organization surveys engagement. A school measures academic outcomes. A community tracks participation rates. Each metric captures something real, but none captures the underlying pattern that produces it. What distinguishes flourishing analysis from conventional culture audits is attention to cross-element alignment—the degree to which values, norms, peer relationships, leadership, structural touchpoints, and social climate are pulling in the same direction or working at cross-purposes. The gap between what a culture says it values and what it actually rewards is often where the most important diagnostic information lives.

This chapter outlines practical techniques for analyzing flourishing within any culture or subculture—whether a family, workplace, school, community organization, professional field, or society at large. It builds on the six cultural elements introduced earlier in the book:

1. Shared Values
2. Norms
3. Peer Support
4. Leadership Support
5. Cultural Touchpoints
6. Social Climate

The goal is not to judge or condemn but to diagnose and understand. Analysis is the first step toward intentional cultivation.

I. Clarifying the Standard: What Do We Mean by Flourishing?

Before analyzing a culture, we must define what we are measuring it against. Analysis without a clear standard devolves into preference. Some aspects of culture will look good to some observers and problematic to others, and without a shared evaluative framework, the conversation goes nowhere. Analysis grounded in shared flourishing values becomes constructive and forward-looking.

Throughout this book, flourishing has been grounded in six core values: productive work, health, joy, kindness, learning, and connection. These values provide the evaluative framework. Every cultural analysis begins with a simple but demanding question:

To what extent do our current cultural patterns reliably support these six forms of thriving?

The word "reliably" matters. Every culture produces instances of flourishing. The diagnostic question is whether the culture consistently and equitably produces flourishing—for most people, most of the time—or whether it produces flourishing for some while quietly undermining it for others. This question applies at every scale, from a family examining its daily rhythms to a society examining its institutions.

II. Multi-Level Cultural Analysis

Culture operates on multiple levels simultaneously, and effective analysis must consider all of them. The formal level—policies, incentive systems, organization charts—is the most visible and easiest to document, but it's rarely where culture truly exists. The informal level—norms, peer behaviors, unspoken expectations—has a much stronger influence on daily experience than any written policy. The symbolic level—the stories shared, the role models, the rituals that emphasize what matters—shapes the emotional significance people assign to their work and connections. The emotional level—the social environment, the general feeling of safety or threat, the presence or absence of hope—is both influenced by the other levels and acts as a force in its own right.

No single metric captures culture. Instead, we look for alignment—or misalignment—across the six cultural elements. The most illuminating findings are often not in any single element but in the patterns between them. Effective analysis, therefore, examines:

- Formal structures (policies, incentives, systems)
- Informal expectations (norms, peer behavior)
- Symbolic signals (stories, role models, rituals)
- Emotional tone (social climate)
- Distribution of power (leadership patterns)

A practical note on scale and access: the techniques described in this chapter differ in their requirements. Some—observational techniques, document review, decision audits—can be performed by anyone with access to publicly available information and the time for careful observation. Others—surveys, focus groups, network mapping—require internal access and participant trust. When starting an analysis, begin with what is accessible. Initial findings from document review and behavioral observation often suffice to generate useful hypotheses that can then be tested with more detailed methods.

III. Analyzing Shared Values

A. Stated vs. Operative Values

Most cultures express admirable values. The real question is whether these values are actually practiced—whether they truly influence decisions when they conflict with other pressures. A culture might claim to value learning and genuinely mean it when conditions are easy. The real test comes when learning becomes inconvenient, when admitting a mistake is risky, or when slowing down to reflect would hurt short-term productivity. Values are truly shown through actions under pressure, not just in mission statements.

The most important thing to understand about values analysis is that the gap between stated and operative values is not necessarily proof of hypocrisy. It often indicates structural misalignment—

while the people leading the culture may genuinely believe in the stated values, the incentive structures, time pressures, and accountability systems in place quietly encourage different behavior. Identifying that gap is the goal of values analysis.

Techniques

1. Document Review

- Mission statements and public messaging
- Policy language and formal guidelines
- Budget allocations (what receives actual resources)

2. Resource Mapping

Observe how time and money are allocated. Consider where discretionary resources actually go when there is competition for them. A culture that claims to value employee health but does not allocate budget to health-supporting programs reveals its true priorities through resource choices rather than words.

- Where is time invested?
- What receives funding under pressure?
- What behaviors are rewarded, and at what cost to other values?

3. Decision Audit

Examine recent high-stakes decisions—the moments when values were most clearly tested. These are especially revealing when they involve trade-offs: when the choice between productivity and health, between short-term gain and long-term learning, or between efficiency and kindness is made explicitly or implicitly.

- What values were prioritized in the final decision?
- What trade-offs were made, and were they acknowledged?
- Whose flourishing was considered, and whose was not?

4. Gap Analysis

Compare stated values to the systems that govern daily experience. The most common gaps are between stated values and compensation systems (does pay reflect what is said to matter?), promotion patterns (who advances, and for what?), recognition structures (what gets publicly celebrated?), and crisis responses (what values are jettisoned first under pressure?).

Flourishing analysis asks: do productive work, health, joy, kindness, learning, and connection consistently influence real priorities, or do they appear primarily in communications?

IV. Analyzing Norms

Norms are the "rules of the game" that guide everyday behavior—the unwritten expectations that people absorb through observation and experience rather than through policy documents. They often determine flourishing more powerfully than formal policies, because they govern the thousand small daily interactions that add up to a cultural reality. A culture can have excellent formal policies on well-being and still have powerful norms that undermine those policies in practice: norms that signal that self-care is weakness, that asking for help is risky, that overwork signals commitment.

Norms often undermine flourishing unintentionally. They develop over time as adaptive responses to real pressures—a workload that genuinely requires long hours, a history of criticism that makes people risk-averse, a competitive environment that erodes trust.

Identifying them requires curiosity rather than accusation. The goal is not to blame those who perpetuate the norms but to understand the conditions that created and sustain them.

A word on method: norms are most reliably identified through observation over time rather than through asking people to describe them. People are often unaware of the norms they operate within, just as fish are unaware of water. What people say the norms are and what the norms actually are may differ significantly.

A. Observational Techniques

1. Behavior Sampling

- How do meetings begin and end? (Are they rushed? Is there space for human exchange?)
- Are people interrupted, and who interrupts whom?
- Are mistakes discussed openly or covered over?

2. Expectation Mapping

- What behaviors are quietly expected but never formally required?
- What happens when someone deviates from the unwritten rules?

3. Boundary Testing (Through Observation)

- What behaviors generate subtle disapproval or social cost?
- What behaviors generate approval, inclusion, or status?

B. Norm Questions for Flourishing

- Are health-supporting behaviors—rest, exercise, help-seeking—normalized or stigmatized?
- Is kindness considered strength or softness?

- Is learning from error encouraged or punished?
- Is overwork subtly glorified as evidence of commitment?
- Is connection treated as essential to the work or as a distraction from it?

V. Analyzing Peer Support

Peer relationships shape daily experience more than policy documents ever will. Whether people feel genuinely supported by their colleagues, whether they can ask for help without fear of judgment, whether their struggles are met with solidarity or indifference—these are among the most powerful determinants of a culture's capacity to support flourishing. And unlike leadership behaviors or formal policies, peer culture is largely self-governing: it reflects the accumulated choices of many individuals, which makes it both more resistant to top-down change and more revealing of the culture's actual values.

Peer support analysis is most useful when it distinguishes between surface-level friendliness and genuine relational safety. Many cultures are warm on the surface while harboring significant undercurrents of competition, judgment, or exclusion. The question is not whether people get along socially, but whether the peer culture creates conditions in which people can be honest about difficulties, ask for help without stigma, and invest in each other's success without feeling that doing so costs them anything.

A. Network Analysis

1. Relational Mapping

- Who talks to whom regularly? Where are the silos?
- Who is isolated or peripheral despite formal inclusion?
- Across which boundaries does support flow, and across which does it stop?

2. *Informal Leaders Identification*

- Whose behavior sets the tone for how others treat each other?
- Who influences morale in ways that formal authority does not capture?

3. *Trust Assessment*

- Do people feel safe asking peers for help without risking their reputation?
- Is confidentiality respected when people share difficulties?
- Are conversations about mental health or personal struggle welcomed or avoided?

B. Peer Culture Indicators

- Do colleagues celebrate each other's progress, or does success generate envy?
- Are setbacks met with support or with subtle judgment?
- Is mentorship visible, accessible, and genuinely generative?
- Are marginalized or newer members integrated into the relational fabric or kept on the periphery?

Flourishing cultures treat peer support as a shared responsibility rather than a private burden. The analysis question is whether the peer culture has developed norms that actively sustain that responsibility, or whether support is left to individual goodwill without structural reinforcement.

VI. Analyzing Leadership Support

Leadership shapes culture not only through decisions and policies but through the constant, low-visibility signal of behavior. What leaders actually do under pressure—not what they say they do, and not what they do when being observed—is the most reliable cultural signal available. A leader who publicly champions work-life balance but sends emails at midnight and schedules meetings on weekends is not consciously undermining a stated value; they are expressing an operative one. People in the culture read these signals accurately and adapt to them.

The most important distinction in leadership analysis is between high-visibility and low-visibility behavior. Leaders are often very intentional about their behavior in public contexts—in town halls, in performance reviews, in moments of crisis that they know are being watched. The more revealing data comes from how they behave in ordinary moments: how they respond when someone raises a concern in a small meeting, how they talk about absent colleagues, how they handle the hundred small daily transactions that nobody is formally tracking.

A second important distinction is between accountability and blame. A culture that holds leaders accountable to flourishing metrics—where leadership behavior is regularly examined against shared values—is different from a culture that blames individual leaders when things go wrong. The former creates conditions for learning; the latter creates conditions for concealment.

A. Leadership Signal Analysis

- What behaviors do leaders model in low-visibility moments, not just formal ones?
- How do leaders respond to stress, failure, and dissent?
- What gets public praise, and what gets ignored or deflected?
- Do leaders model the same flourishing behaviors they ask of others?

B. Power and Accountability Review

- Are leaders accountable to flourishing metrics, or only to performance metrics?
- Do leaders actively invite dissent, or does the culture of deference suppress honest feedback?
- Is stewardship—serving the conditions for others' flourishing—emphasized over dominance?
- Are leaders transparent about the trade-offs they are making?

C. Leadership Consistency Test

Flourishing requires congruence between what leaders say and what they do. Do leaders' daily behaviors align with the values of health, learning, connection, kindness, and sustainable productivity? Cultural trust erodes when leadership signals contradict declared values—not all at once, but gradually, as people accumulate evidence that the stated values are not the operative ones.

VII. Analyzing Cultural Touchpoints

Touchpoints are the structural mechanisms through which a culture transmits its values and reinforces behavior over time. They include rewards and recognition systems, hiring and onboarding practices, performance evaluation criteria, training and development programs, promotion patterns, physical space design, and the stories that get told about who succeeds and why. Touchpoints are the most durable elements of culture—they often outlast the people who created them and continue to shape behavior long after the original intentions have been forgotten.

The critical insight for touchpoint analysis is that touchpoints do not communicate what the culture intends—they communicate what the culture actually does. A performance review system that evaluates only quantitative output shows that quantitative output matters, regardless of what the organization says about the importance of collaboration or learning. A hiring process that screens only for technical competence communicates that technical competence is the primary value, regardless of stated commitments to relational culture. Misaligned touchpoints quietly undermine stated values, often in ways that no one has consciously designed and that accumulate invisibly over time.

Physical space design is worth noting, as it is frequently overlooked in cultural analysis. Space communicates hierarchy, privacy norms, and the value placed on different activities. An open-plan office with no quiet space signals a lack of value for focused work and introversion. A building in which leadership occupies a separate, bounded space communicates something about accessibility and hierarchy. These signals are ambient—people absorb them without necessarily articulating them.

A. Incentive Mapping

- What behaviors are materially rewarded? Which go unrewarded?
- What behaviors reliably advance careers, and what behaviors stall them?
- What behaviors receive public acknowledgment, and what goes unrecognized?

B. Onboarding Review

- What do newcomers learn about "how things really work" in their first weeks?

- Are flourishing values embedded in onboarding from the start, or only in formal orientation materials?

C. Reinforcement Alignment

Flourishing analysis examines whether touchpoints consistently reinforce long-term health over short-term output, collaboration over internal competition, learning over perfectionism, and connection over fragmentation. The question to ask of each major touchpoint is: if someone wanted to thrive in this culture, what behavior would this touchpoint teach them to display?

VIII. Analyzing Social Climate

Social climate is the emotional weather of a culture—the ambient sense of trust, safety, hope, and belonging that people carry with them through their daily experience. It is both a product of the other five cultural elements and a force in its own right. A culture with strong stated values, reasonable norms, and well-designed touchpoints can still foster a corrosive social climate if those elements are perceived as hollow or applied inconsistently. Conversely, a culture with structural imperfections can still have a genuinely supportive climate if the relational fabric is strong enough to buffer them.

Social climate is often the clearest leading indicator of underlying cultural alignment. When climate deteriorates—when hope gives way to cynicism, when trust erodes, when people begin to experience belonging as conditional—it is usually a signal that one or more of the other cultural elements has fallen out of alignment, often before that misalignment shows up in more visible metrics like turnover or performance. Climate assessment is, therefore, not just a measure of how people feel; it is an early warning system for cultural drift.

A critical methodological note: social climate cannot be accurately assessed through anonymous surveys alone. Surveys are useful for identifying patterns and for ensuring that minority experiences are captured. Still, they are vulnerable to performative responding—people reporting the climate they feel they should report rather than the one they actually experience. The most reliable climate assessments combine survey data with structured listening conversations, attention to behavioral patterns (is humor cynical or generous? do people protect or undermine each other?), and longitudinal tracking that can detect change over time.

A. Climate Assessment Methods

1. Survey Tools

- Belonging measures
- Psychological safety scales
- Engagement indicators
- Burnout markers

2. Focus Groups and Listening Sessions

- Narrative sharing and experience mapping
- Story analysis: what stories get told, and what do they signal about what is safe to say?
- Attention to what does not get said as well as what does

3. Sentiment Patterns

Informal conversation is one of the most reliable indicators of climate. What emotions dominate the ambient culture? Is humor generous or cynical? Is hope realistic and grounded in credible action, or has it become performative—the language of hope maintained while the conditions for hope have eroded?

B. Climate Alignment Questions

Do people feel valued for more than their productivity? Is there a shared purpose that extends beyond individual self-interest? Do individuals feel genuinely seen by their colleagues and leaders? Is hope grounded in credible action, or has it become formulaic?

IX. Integrative Cultural Diagnosis: Finding the Patterns That Matter

After analyzing each element separately, the most important work begins: integration. The goal of flourishing analysis is not to produce a balanced scorecard across six elements but to identify the specific patterns of alignment and misalignment that shape daily experience. Culture functions like an interconnected web: a change in one strand creates tension or slack in others, and the system tends to maintain its overall pattern even when individual elements are adjusted. This is why isolated interventions—a new recognition program, a leadership training, a revised policy—so often fail to produce lasting change. The pattern, not the element, is the unit of analysis.

The following cross-element patterns frequently appear in organizations that are struggling to flourish. They are worth looking for deliberately, because each is both common and easily misread when elements are examined in isolation:

Strong stated values, weak touchpoint reinforcement. This is perhaps the most common pattern. The values are genuine—people across the culture would describe them sincerely if asked—but the structural mechanisms that should reinforce them (recognition systems, promotion criteria, performance evaluation, resource allocation) reward different behavior. Over time, this creates a persistent gap between the culture people aspire to and the culture they actually inhabit. The result is often a specific kind of cynicism: people do not disbelieve the values; they disbelieve that the values will be honored in the moments that matter.

Supportive peers, misaligned leadership signals. Peer culture can be genuinely warm and collaborative, while leadership behavior signals something quite different. When this pattern is present, the peer community provides real support but also real protection—people learn to shield the things that matter to them from leadership visibility, which means they also shield honest information from upward communication. The culture becomes bifurcated: one reality for the people doing the work, another reality for the people directing it.

Positive climate in pockets, systemic inequity in rewards. A culture can have a healthy social climate in specific subgroups—a department with a strong manager, a team with a long history of working together—while the broader reward and recognition systems distribute opportunity and recognition inequitably. This pattern is often invisible to those in the well-functioning pockets, who reasonably experience the culture as supportive, while those outside the pockets experience something quite different. It produces genuine disagreement within the culture about what the culture is.

Healthy norms, overwhelming structural demands. A culture can have good norms around support, learning, and connection and still produce burnout and disengagement if the structural demands placed on people—workload, pace, resource scarcity—are too high to allow those norms to be enacted. People want to support each other, learn from mistakes, and invest in connection, but there is no time for it. The norms are present in values and intention; the structure prevents them from being present in behavior. This pattern is particularly insidious because it can be experienced as individual failure ("I should be doing better at this") rather than as a structural problem.

When these patterns are identified, they should be named precisely. The diagnostic report is not "our culture has problems with X" but "our culture has strong X and Y, but the relationship between Y and Z is producing W, which means that..." The more specific the diagnosis, the more useful the intervention.

X. Quantitative and Qualitative Measurement

A flourishing analysis combines quantitative and qualitative data, and the combination matters. Numbers identify patterns at scale—they can reveal that a problem is more widespread than qualitative conversation suggests, or more localized, or concentrated in a specific subgroup. Stories explain patterns—they surface the causal logic connecting structural conditions to lived experience and identify the specific mechanisms through which cultural elements interact. Numbers alone produce findings that no one knows how to act on. Stories alone produce findings that may not generalize. Together, the two produce findings that are both credible and actionable.

Quantitative Indicators

1. Health metrics (reported well-being, sick days, stress indicators)
2. Retention rates and exit interview patterns
3. Burnout prevalence and trend over time
4. Engagement scores, disaggregated by subgroup
5. Absenteeism patterns
6. Conflict frequency and resolution patterns
7. Participation in voluntary learning and development

Qualitative Indicators

1. Stories of support and of being let down
2. Narratives of moral injury (moments when the culture required people to act against their values)
3. Perceived fairness and consistency of leadership
4. Descriptions of where people feel genuinely valued vs. instrumentalized
5. Language patterns: what words are used to describe success, failure, difficulty, and care?

One particularly useful qualitative technique is to ask people to describe a moment when the culture was at its best—and a moment when it fell short. The contrast between these two stories is often more diagnostic than any survey score.

XI. Participatory Cultural Analysis

Flourishing analysis itself should model flourishing values. The way an analysis is conducted—who is included, whose perspectives are solicited, how findings are reported, what happens with the results—communicates as much as the content of the findings. An analysis conducted by a small group of leaders and reported to the same group without broader participation reinforces the very patterns of hierarchy and exclusion that may be undermining flourishing. An analysis conducted with genuine cross-level participation, transparent reporting, and shared interpretation builds the relational trust that is itself a condition for cultural change.

The principle of participatory analysis also reflects an epistemic reality: the people most affected by a culture are often the most accurate observers of it. People in positions of authority typically have less accurate models of the culture they oversee than people who experience it daily from less powerful positions. Structures that include voices from across the hierarchy—particularly those with the least power and most to lose from honesty—produce more accurate diagnoses and more durable solutions.

Effective participatory strategies include:

Cross-level working groups in which people from different positions in the hierarchy analyze the same data together, surfacing where their interpretations diverge and examining what those divergences reveal. Anonymous input channels that allow people to share observations and experiences without the social risk of identification. Transparent reporting of findings to the people who participated, not only to leadership. Shared interpretation sessions in which findings are discussed collectively before conclusions are drawn. Action research cycles in which participants are involved not just in the analysis but in designing and evaluating the interventions that follow.

XII. Ongoing Action Research

Culture is dynamic. Pressures, events, personnel changes, and the accumulating weight of individual decisions shape it. A culture that was genuinely flourishing five years ago may have drifted under new leadership, new competitive pressures, or the aftereffects of a crisis. A struggling culture may have improved through sustained attention and intentional change. This means that flourishing analysis cannot be a one-time event; it must be an ongoing practice.

The most useful framework for ongoing cultural analysis is action research, originally articulated by Kurt Lewin, whose work emphasized that lasting social change requires collaborative inquiry and iterative refinement. Action research treats analysis and change as inseparable: the analysis is designed not just to produce knowledge but to produce knowledge that the people doing it can act on. The cycle is:

- Assess: gather systematic data on current cultural patterns
- Reflect: interpret findings collaboratively, testing initial hypotheses against the data
- Adjust: design and implement specific changes in response to findings
- Re-assess: measure whether the changes produced the intended effects
- Share learning: communicate findings and adaptations across the culture

The fifth step—sharing learning—is frequently omitted, yet arguably the most important. A culture that learns from its own analysis and shares that learning builds the organizational intelligence and collective self-awareness that makes future change increasingly effective. Flourishing cultures become learning cultures.

XIII. Warning Signs of Cultural Misalignment

During analysis, several recurring patterns may signal that a culture is drifting away from flourishing. These warning signs are worth naming explicitly because they are often present in plain sight but go unaddressed—either because they have been normalized over time or because addressing them would require confronting uncomfortable systemic realities.

Chronic overextension framed as dedication. When exhaustion becomes a signal of commitment rather than a cost to be managed, the culture has begun to treat human depletion as a resource. This pattern is self-reinforcing: those who set limits are seen as less committed, making limit-setting socially costly and deepening exhaustion throughout the culture.

Rising isolation despite digital connectivity. When people report feeling more alone even as communication technologies multiply, it usually signals that the quality of relational connection has deteriorated even as its frequency has increased. Superficial connection—many interactions, little depth or trust—can produce an experience of isolation that is more disorienting than ordinary loneliness because it is harder to name.

Cynicism is normalized as sophistication. When the expression of hope or genuine care becomes associated with naïveté, the culture has lost its capacity for the kind of honest engagement that makes collective effort possible. Cynicism protects against disappointment, but it also protects against the vulnerability that genuine connection and genuine effort require.

Leadership distance from daily realities. When leaders consistently operate with inaccurate models of what is actually happening in the culture—because honest feedback has been blocked, because their position insulates them from daily experience, or because they have stopped paying attention—their decisions will consistently misfire in ways they cannot diagnose. This pattern is especially dangerous because it tends to produce confident leadership of the wrong things.

Reward systems favor short-term gains. When a culture consistently rewards short-term productivity at the cost of long-term health, learning, and relationships, it is depleting its own foundations. The costs are usually invisible in the short term and catastrophic in the long term.

Learning is treated as remedial rather than developmental. When training and development are primarily associated with addressing deficits rather than with ongoing growth, the culture signals that learning is for people who are failing rather than for everyone. This association suppresses the willingness to acknowledge gaps and to ask for help, which is essential to a genuine learning culture.

Identifying these signals early allows correction before a crisis. Each is also a diagnostic finding: its presence indicates which specific elements and patterns to examine more closely.

XIV. From Diagnosis to Cultivation

The purpose of analysis is not critique—it is cultivation. A diagnosis that does not lead to action is not neutral; it raises expectations and then frustrates them, which makes the next attempt at cultural change harder. The transition from diagnosis to cultivation is therefore not a separate phase that follows analysis but something that must be built into the analysis process from the beginning: the people conducting the analysis should be thinking from the start about what kind of intervention the findings will support, and the people who will need to act on the findings should be involved in producing them.

A good diagnostic report concludes with more than findings. It concludes with a clear-eyed account of what is working—specifically, what cultural patterns are genuinely supporting flourishing and should be protected and amplified—alongside a specific account of the misalignments that most need attention. Not everything can be addressed at once; in fact, trying to do so is one of the most reliable ways to ensure that nothing actually changes. A well-designed diagnostic report is, therefore, also a prioritization tool.

Prioritizing among misalignments requires judgment about two things: which misalignments are producing the most harm, and which are most amenable to change given current conditions. These are not always the same. The most harmful misalignment may be deeply structural and require sustained effort over years; a less harmful misalignment may be addressable quickly and in ways that build the trust and momentum needed for harder work. A good cultivation plan often begins with the latter, not because the former is less important but because visible early progress is itself a cultural intervention—it demonstrates that change is possible and that the analysis was not merely performative.

Communicating findings requires as much care as producing them. Findings presented in ways that create defensiveness tend to produce defensive responses rather than change. Findings framed as systemic patterns rather than individual failures, and delivered in contexts that invite genuine engagement rather than passive reception, are more likely to generate the shared commitment that cultural change requires. The analysis should be presented as a shared resource, not as a verdict.

A complete diagnostic report should conclude with:

- Clear strengths to preserve and amplify, with specific examples of what is working and why
- Specific misalignments to address, named precisely enough that the analysis can inform concrete decisions
- A prioritized sequence of intervention points, distinguishing between quick wins and longer-horizon work
- Measurable flourishing goals, so that progress can be tracked and the next analysis cycle has a baseline
- Shared accountability structures that distribute responsibility for follow-through across multiple roles rather than concentrating it in a single function

- A connection back to the four-phase change process in the next chapter, so that diagnostic findings translate directly into the analysis, objective setting, and leadership development work that Phase I requires

When cultures learn to examine themselves honestly and compassionately—with the same curiosity and care they would want directed at any complex system they were trying to improve—they begin to move from surviving to thriving.

Conclusion: Seeing Clearly to Build Wisely

Cultural forces shape our mental health, relationships, institutions, and opportunities. Without deliberate analysis, these forces operate by default—rewarding and punishing, connecting and isolating, enabling and undermining, largely below the threshold of collective awareness.

With thoughtful examination—of values, norms, peers, leadership, touchpoints, and climate—we gain the capacity to see these forces clearly and to design environments that reliably support productive work, health, joy, kindness, learning, and connection. The analysis described in this chapter is not a technical exercise; it is an act of care for the people who inhabit the culture, and for the purposes the culture is meant to serve.

Flourishing does not emerge accidentally.

It emerges when cultures learn to see themselves clearly—and then choose alignment.

Chapter 19

Embracing Systemic and Systematic Change

CULTURE CHANGE IS often imagined as something that should happen quickly—through a new policy, a bold announcement, or a charismatic leader. When these efforts fail, people sometimes conclude that culture is either too vague or too entrenched to be deliberately changed. In reality, the opposite is true. Culture can be shaped—but only when its complexity is taken seriously.

Cultures are complex systems composed of multiple interacting elements: shared values, norms, peer relationships, leadership practices, social climate, and cultural touchpoints. These elements reinforce one another over time, which is precisely why culture is so powerful—and why it resists simple, single-solution approaches. Changing one element in isolation rarely produces lasting results. People adapt around the change, compensate for misalignment, or wait for the initiative to fade.

The most effective approach to co-creating a flourishing society is to treat culture change as a **systematic, iterative process**—one that unfolds over time, engages people as participants rather than targets, and aligns daily experience with flourishing values. Most meaningful cultural change follows a four-phase process.

Two words in the chapter title are worth distinguishing. "Systemic" describes the kind of change this chapter advocates: change that addresses the whole web of interconnected cultural elements rather than isolated behaviors or single initiatives. "Systematic" describes how to pursue it: through a deliberate, phased process rather than through heroic individual effort. Both are necessary. Systemic thinking without a systematic process produces good intentions that stall. A systematic process without systemic thinking produces orderly activity that does not reach the roots. Chapter 17 addressed where to begin—how to assess social climate and identify the best entry point for change. This chapter addresses how to proceed once that starting point has been chosen.

Operating Principles: How to Approach the Work

The four-phase process described below provides the structural map for culture change. But a map does not tell you how to walk—the orientation, pace, and spirit you bring to the work matter as much as the sequence. These twelve principles are not steps in a process; they are the mindsets and disciplines that should infuse every step. A change effort that mechanically follows the four phases but violates these principles—by mandating rather than modeling, by measuring without protecting privacy, by celebrating too loudly, too soon—will produce compliance at best and cynicism at worst. The principles and the process work together.

1. Begin with an Honest Assessment (*see Chapter 19 for recommendations*)

Ground your initiative in reality. Build from an accurate understanding of strengths, tensions, and existing cultural patterns.

2. Build on Strength

Amplify what already supports flourishing. Expansion is more powerful than condemnation.

3. Address Systems, not Blame

When problems surface, examine the conditions shaping behavior. Sustainable change adjusts structures, norms, and incentives—not just individuals.

4. Engage People as Co-Creators

Invite meaningful participation. Consultation builds trust; involvement builds ownership.

5. Align Words with Structures

Ensure that values are reinforced through rewards, recognition, evaluation, storytelling, and daily practices. Symbolic language without structural support erodes credibility.

6. Move at the Speed of Trust

Progress must be paced according to relational credibility. Where trust is weak, prioritize listening and consistency.

7. Model Before You Mandate

Leaders signal priorities through behavior. Integrity, humility, and transparency create permission for change.

8. Protect Psychological Safety

Safeguard confidentiality, respectful dialogue, and responsible data use. Safety enables honesty and learning.

9. Pursue Measurable Progress

Define clear objectives, track meaningful indicators, and celebrate improvement. Flourishing grows incrementally.

10. Reinforce Through Celebration and Story

Publicly recognize progress. Stories and rituals strengthen norms and shared identity.

11. Approach Resistance with Curiosity

Listen for underlying concerns and competing pressures. Curiosity reduces polarization.

12. Commit to Renewal

Plan for reassessment and reintegration. Flourishing must become identity—not a temporary campaign.

The Four-Phase Culture Change Process

With the operating principles in mind, the four-phase process below provides a step-by-step approach to culture change. Each phase is sequenced deliberately: the analysis and leadership work of Phase I creates the foundation that makes genuine involvement in Phase II possible; the buy-in built in Phase II creates the conditions for the structural integration of Phase III to be embraced rather than resisted; and the evaluation and renewal work of Phase IV ensures that what was built does not gradually drift back to old patterns. Each phase is organized around a small number of essential planning questions—questions that deserve honest answers before proceeding.

Phase I: Analysis, Objective Setting, and Leadership Development

Preparing the Soil

Before launching visible change efforts, assess the cultural ground in which those efforts will grow.

The most common cause of culture change failure is not a flawed vision or an inadequate strategy—it is launching into action before the conditions for success are in place. Phase I exists to prevent that. It asks three foundational questions: Is the soil ready? What are we trying to grow? And who will tend it? The answers—about social climate, specific objectives, and leadership readiness—shape every subsequent decision. Investing time here is not a delay; it is the most efficient path to durable change.

1. What is the current cultural reality?

Is there an adequately supportive social climate—characterized by community, shared direction, and realistic hope—to support cooperative change?

One way to assess this is through the Social Climate Assessment described in Chapter 17. If the social climate is weak in one or more subcultures, you face an important decision:

- Begin by strengthening the climate ("preparing the soil"), or
- Start in subcultures where climate strengths already exist, and momentum can build.

Flourishing initiatives often fail not because the vision is flawed but because the soil is not ready. A weak social climate quietly resists cooperative change. Investing in trust, shared meaning, and psychological safety may be the most strategic first step.

2. What specific flourishing objectives will you pursue?

You cannot change everything at once. Which flourishing values expressed in attitudes and behavior need the most attention? How will we "walk the talk" when it comes to:

- Productive Work
- Health
- Joy
- Kindness
- Learning
- Connection

Define a small number of measurable objectives. Clear goals prevent diffusion of effort and increase credibility.

3. Who will lead—and are they prepared?

Cultural change requires both positional and relational leadership.

- Authority leaders (executives, managers, board members) provide legitimacy and structural alignment.
- Peer leaders provide credibility and cultural translation.

Usually, a combination of both is essential.

But authority alone is insufficient. Planning must consider:

- Do people trust these leaders?
- Are leaders prepared to model flourishing values?
- Do they have time, authority, and support?
- Are they aligned with one another?

Leadership development is not a side task—it is foundational soil preparation.

Phase II: Involvement

Creating Shared Ownership

Once objectives and leadership are clarified, the initiative must expand beyond a small planning group.

Culture doesn't have to be something that happens to people; it can be something people carry and enact together. This means culture change cannot be designed by a small group and then imposed on everyone else. Phase II involves genuine co-creation: explaining what the initiative is and why it matters, creating structured opportunities for members to shape it, and identifying early wins that build momentum and show that change is real. The order is important: involvement should come before structural integration. People who helped design the effort are much more likely to sustain and advocate for the system changes that Phase III will require.

4. How will you explain the initiative?

Your message should clearly articulate:

- What the effort is
- Why it matters
- How it will unfold

Tailor the message to the language, values, and pressures of the subculture. A hospital, a school district, a small business, and a civic organization will each require different framing.

Highlight the benefits that resonate most:

- Reduced stress
- Stronger collaboration
- Greater meaning

- Higher engagement
- Improved outcomes

Clarity builds trust. Transparency reduces resistance.

5. How will people be meaningfully involved?

Flourishing cannot be mandated. It must be co-created.

Consider:

- Listening sessions
- Surveys
- Small-group dialogues
- Cross-functional task groups
- Pilot initiatives

People support what they help design. Early involvement builds ownership and surfaces hidden strengths and concerns.

6. Where can early wins occur?

Visible progress generates momentum.

Identify areas where:

- leadership support is strong,
- climate is relatively healthy, and
- measurable improvements are feasible.

Early successes increase confidence that change is possible and strengthen belief in leadership competence.

Phase III: Integration of Cultural Supports

Aligning the Web

Cultural change becomes durable when multiple strands of the web reinforce new patterns.

The single most common reason culture change stalls after a promising start is that new values are articulated but not structurally reinforced. People hear the message, agree with it, and then return to environments where the incentives, recognition systems, and daily routines still reward the old behavior. Phase III addresses this follow-through directly. It asks which elements of the cultural web need to shift to support your objectives, and whether the formal systems—performance reviews, hiring criteria, meeting structures, communication channels—reinforce or contradict what you are building. Integration is what converts good intentions into lived culture.

7. Which cultural elements must shift?

Consider each of the six elements:

- Values
- Norms
- Peer support
- Leadership behaviors
- Social climate
- Cultural touchpoints (rewards, modeling, storytelling, training, hiring, evaluation, etc.)

Which elements must be intentionally adjusted to support your objectives?

For example:

- If peer support is a goal, are there structured opportunities for peer connection?
- If kindness is a value, is it recognized and rewarded?
- If learning is emphasized, are mistakes treated as learning opportunities?

Integration prevents change from becoming symbolic rather than structural.

8. Are systems aligned?

Examine formal systems:

- Performance reviews
- Incentives
- Hiring practices
- Meeting structures
- Communication channels

If these systems contradict flourishing values, change efforts will stall. Planning must include alignment.

Phase IV: Evaluation, Celebration, and Renewal

Stabilizing and Sustaining Change

Cultural change is not an event—it is an ongoing process of learning and renewal.

A culture change initiative that never formally evaluates its progress will drift. Without measurement, it is impossible to know whether the effort is working or whether early enthusiasm is masking underlying stagnation. Without celebration, the people doing the hard daily work of culture change do not receive the signal that their effort is noticed and valued. Without renewal, even successful culture change slowly reverts as new people join, as pressures shift, and as the original energy fades. Phase IV is not a wrap-up; it determines whether the work of the previous three phases becomes permanent.

9. How will progress be measured?

Measurement increases credibility and learning.

Possible metrics include:

- Social Climate Indicator scores
- Engagement surveys

- Retention data
- Absenteeism
- Psychological safety indicators
- Qualitative narratives

Measurement should be transparent and respectful of privacy. Trust depends on confidentiality and responsible use of data.

10. How will success be celebrated?

Celebration is not superficial. It reinforces norms and signals priority.

- Public recognition
- Storytelling
- Rituals
- Milestone acknowledgments

Celebration strengthens positive emotional climate and encourages continued effort.

11. How will renewal occur?

Cultures drift unless renewed.

Plan for:

- Periodic reassessment
- Leadership refreshment
- Integration into onboarding
- Ongoing dialogue

Flourishing becomes sustainable when it shifts from initiative to identity.

Strategic Considerations Across All Phases

In addition to phase-specific questions, planners should consider:

- What resistance is likely—and what values or fears underlie it?
- Are there competing initiatives that could dilute focus?
- What myths and misunderstandings need to be debunked?
- Is the organization in crisis, transition, or stability?
- How will psychological safety and confidentiality be protected?
- What existing cultural strengths can be amplified rather than replaced?

Effective planning honors the system's reality while guiding it toward possibility.

Planning Checklist

The checklist below is designed to be used before launching each phase of the initiative—not as a test to pass but as a structured prompt for honest reflection. It is most useful when completed collaboratively by the planning group, since disagreements about whether an item is truly complete are often as informative as the items themselves. You do not need perfect answers to every question, but you should have thoughtful responses to most. Items left blank are an agenda for the work ahead. Use this checklist to guide your planning before launching your initiative.

Phase I: Analysis, Objective Setting, and Leadership Development

Preparing the Soil

Cultural Assessment

☐ Have we assessed the current social climate (community, shared direction, realistic hope)?

☐ Do we understand which subcultures are stronger or weaker?

☐ Have we identified existing cultural strengths we can build upon?
☐ Are there obvious cultural misalignments that need attention?

Clear Objectives
☐ Have we defined 2–4 specific flourishing objectives?
☐ Are these objectives realistic and measurable?
☐ Do we know which cultural elements (values, norms, peer support, leadership, touchpoints, climate) must shift to support them?
☐ Have we prioritized rather than trying to change everything at once?

Leadership Readiness
☐ Have we identified both authority leaders and peer leaders?
☐ Do these leaders have credibility and trust?
☐ Are leaders aligned with one another?
☐ Have leaders been prepared to model flourishing values?
☐ Do leaders have time and structural support to lead effectively?

Phase II: Involvement

Creating Shared Ownership
Communication and Framing
☐ Have we clearly articulated what this initiative is?
☐ Have we explained why it matters in language that resonates locally?
☐ Have we described how the initiative will unfold?
☐ Are we transparent about goals, expectations, and timelines?

Participation Strategy

☐ Have we created opportunities for listening and dialogue?
☐ Will people have meaningful roles in shaping the initiative?
☐ Have we identified early adopters or champions?
☐ Have we planned for early, visible wins?

Phase III: Integration of Cultural Supports

Aligning the Web

Alignment of Cultural Elements

☐ Are flourishing values clearly articulated?
☐ Are norms being clarified or strengthened?
☐ Are peer support structures in place?
☐ Are leaders modeling the desired culture?
☐ Is the social climate being actively nurtured?
☐ Are cultural touchpoints (rewards, recognition, storytelling, training, evaluation) reinforcing the change?

Systems Alignment

☐ Do performance systems reinforce flourishing behaviors?
☐ Are incentives aligned with stated values?
☐ Are hiring and onboarding processes supportive of the desired culture?
☐ Do meeting structures and communication channels support connection and learning?

Phase IV: Evaluation, Celebration, and Renewal

Stabilizing and Sustaining Change

Measurement

☐ Have we selected meaningful indicators of progress?
☐ Are we collecting both quantitative and qualitative data?

☐ Are privacy and confidentiality being protected?
☐ Are results communicated transparently?

Celebration
☐ Are we recognizing early progress?
☐ Are we sharing stories of positive change?
☐ Are leaders publicly reinforcing success?

Renewal
☐ Have we scheduled periodic reassessment?
☐ Are we integrating flourishing principles into onboarding and leadership development?
☐ Is this initiative becoming part of our identity rather than a temporary project?

Strategic Readiness Reflection
Before launching, ask:
☐ Is this the right time?
☐ Are there competing priorities that could undermine focus?
☐ Is there sufficient trust to support honest dialogue?
☐ Are we prepared for resistance—and ready to listen?
☐ Are we committed to a multi-phase process rather than a quick fix?

Final Readiness Question
If someone asked, *"Why will this succeed here?"*
Could you answer with clarity and confidence?
If yes, you are ready to begin cultivating.

Planning as Stewardship

A flourishing culture should be cultivated intentionally.

Planning is the disciplined practice of stewardship—examining the soil, selecting priorities, developing leaders, engaging the community, aligning systems, measuring progress, and renewing commitment.

When planning is thoughtful and systematic, cultural change becomes less about heroic effort and more about adjusting conditions so that flourishing becomes the natural expression of daily life.

Chapter 20

Why Flourishing Cultures Matter: A Summary of Social Benefits and the Case for Urgency

THROUGHOUT THIS BOOK, I built the case that culture is not merely the backdrop against which social life unfolds—it is an active force that shapes what people experience, what they can become, and what problems societies can solve. The preceding chapters have examined how a flourishing culture operates within specific institutions: families, schools, workplaces, civic organizations, healthcare systems, and government. This chapter steps back to take a wider view.

What is at stake when a society either cultivates or neglects cultural conditions for flourishing? The answer, as this chapter documents, is not abstract. It touches the most pressing and costly problems that societies face: mental illness and physical disease, loneliness, crime and violence, racism and social injustice, economic underperformance, and the erosion of effective democratic governance. A flourishing culture does not eliminate these challenges—human life will always include adversity, conflict, and hardship. But it changes the conditions under which people face those challenges and the likelihood that institutions can address them effectively.

This chapter synthesizes the evidence and argument developed across the preceding sections to answer two questions. First: what specific social problems does a flourishing culture help to address, and through what mechanisms? Second: why does the cultivation of flourishing cultures deserve to be treated with the same seriousness and urgency that societies direct toward economic policy, public health, or national security?

Part I: The Social Problems a Flourishing Culture Addresses

The problems cataloged below are not unrelated. They share a common root: the degradation of the cultural conditions—trust, connection, shared purpose, dignity, and mutual accountability—that enable individuals to develop and communities to function. This is why a cultural approach to social problems is not merely one strategy among many. It simultaneously addresses the generative conditions that lie upstream of many specific pathologies.

1. Mental Health

Mental health is often framed as an individual issue, something to be addressed through therapy, medication, or personal resilience. This framing is not wrong, but it is incomplete. A growing body of research establishes that mental health is also powerfully shaped by the cultural environments in which people live—the norms, relationships, institutional practices, and ambient conditions that either support or quietly undermine psychological well-being.

The social philosopher Erich Fromm argued that many psychological struggles reflect not only personal distress but also the pressures of unhealthy social environments. When cultures reward isolation, excessive competition, or chronic insecurity, individuals are more likely to experience anxiety, alienation, and loss of meaning—not because of personal inadequacy but because the environment is producing those responses. Positive psychology researchers, including Martin Seligman, have similarly emphasized that well-being depends on supportive conditions that enable people to develop meaning, a sense of accomplishment, relationships, and positive emotions.

A flourishing culture addresses mental health at the level of its generative conditions. When communities consistently emphasize productive work, health, joy, kindness, learning, and connection, they create everyday environments that reinforce psychological well-being. People experience greater belonging and purpose. Relationships become more supportive. Institutions operate in ways that respect dignity and encourage growth. This does not mean that mental health challenges disappear—but it means that individuals facing difficulty are more likely to encounter empathy rather than stigma, resources rather than barriers, and community rather than isolation.

Flourishing cultures function, in this sense, as psychological infrastructure: a system of social support that quietly strengthens mental health across the population, reducing the downstream demand on clinical systems by addressing conditions before they become crises.

2. Physical Health and Disease Prevention

The relationship between culture and physical health is less obvious than that between culture and mental health, but it is no less real. Cultures shape the behaviors, relationships, and environments that either protect or erode health. People in flourishing communities are more likely to maintain healthy habits, seek preventive care, support one another during illness, and participate in communities that promote physical activity and positive relationships.

Dean Ornish's research has highlighted the powerful role that social connection and supportive relationships play not only in reducing disease risk but in improving recovery from illness. Chronic isolation and chronic stress—both products of cultural conditions as much as individual circumstances—are now understood to be significant contributors to cardiovascular disease, immune dysfunction, and accelerated aging. The cultural environment is, in this sense, a powerful determinant of health.

A flourishing society functions not only as a mechanism for treating disease but as a cultural environment that strengthens resilience and healing across the population. Healthcare systems, workplaces, families, and communities that reinforce the conditions for flourishing are also necessarily engaged in disease prevention—even when that is not their stated purpose. The public health implications of this insight are significant: cultural investment is health investment.

3. Loneliness and Social Isolation

Loneliness has become one of the defining social conditions of contemporary life in many developed societies. Research by Julianne Holt-Lunstad has established that strong social relationships significantly improve well-being. At the same time, the health risks associated with loneliness and isolation are comparable to those of smoking and obesity. Yet loneliness is typically addressed—when it is addressed at all—as an individual problem, something for isolated individuals to solve on their own.

A flourishing culture approaches loneliness differently: as a signal that the cultural conditions for connection have weakened, and that the solution lies in restoring those conditions and encouraging isolated individuals to reach out. When societies emphasize values of kindness, inclusion, and genuine participation, social norms shift in ways that make reaching out easier and more likely to be reciprocated. Institutions and communities that actively create opportunities for people to interact, collaborate, and support one another build the relational infrastructure within which connection becomes possible and normal.

The distinction between a society that addresses loneliness clinically—treating it as a symptom in individuals who present with it—and a society that addresses it culturally—by cultivating the conditions in which belonging is produced and sustained—is the difference between treating a disease and removing its causes. Flourishing cultures work to address the causes of loneliness and support individual agency in developing relationships.

4. Crime and Violence

The relationship between culture and crime is well-established in sociological research. Robert J. Sampson's work on collective efficacy—the degree to which community members trust one another and are willing to act on behalf of shared goals—has demonstrated that communities with higher levels of trust, mutual support, and shared expectations are substantially better able to maintain public safety and reduce violence, independent of economic conditions. Culture, not just poverty, shapes crime rates.

A flourishing culture addresses crime and violence through several distinct mechanisms. Strong relationships among neighbors, families, and peers create informal systems of support and accountability that discourage destructive behavior and provide constructive alternatives. People who feel a genuine sense of belonging, purpose, and responsibility to others are less likely to harm those others. Communities with high social cohesion are better able to recognize and respond to problems before they escalate.

Flourishing cultures also change the conditions under which rehabilitation and reintegration are possible. A community that extends genuine belonging to those who have caused harm—not naïve acceptance but the possibility of reintegration into a community of mutual accountability—creates conditions under which lasting change is more likely than one that responds to crime primarily through exclusion and punishment. The cultural infrastructure of belonging is, in this sense, also the infrastructure of public safety.

5. Racism and Social Injustice

Racism and social injustice are sustained not only by explicit prejudice and deliberate discrimination but by cultural patterns—norms, institutions, narratives, and embedded assumptions—that distribute dignity, opportunity, and safety unequally across groups. Addressing these patterns requires cultural change, not only legal or policy reform, because the cultural patterns that sustain inequality often persist long after the formal rules that originally produced them have been changed.

Social psychologist Gordon W. Allport's contact hypothesis established that positive, cooperative contact between groups—especially when supported by fair norms and institutional backing—can significantly reduce prejudice and discrimination. A flourishing culture creates and sustains the conditions in which such contact is more likely to occur: inclusive institutions, equitable access to opportunity, and cultural norms that encourage people to see one another as fellow members of a shared community rather than as competitors or outsiders.

When communities actively cultivate values of dignity, fairness, kindness, and connection, they reinforce the cultural infrastructure on which justice depends. This does not mean that cultural cultivation is a substitute for structural reform—the two are complementary, and each requires the other. But it does mean that legal and policy changes made without corresponding cultural change will be slower to take effect, more vulnerable to erosion, and less likely to produce the genuine shifts in everyday experience that justice ultimately requires.

6. Economic Performance and Business Resilience

The relationship between culture and economic performance is well-documented but often underweighted in economic policy discussions, which tend to focus on financial and regulatory variables. Research by scholars, including Daniel Coyle, has demonstrated that environments that foster belonging, psychological safety, and shared goals consistently produce stronger performance, more sustained innovation, and greater organizational resilience than environments that rely primarily on incentive structures and formal oversight.

A flourishing culture strengthens economic performance through several mechanisms. Engaged, well-supported employees are more capable of sustained effort, creativity, and effective problem-solving. Cultures characterized by trust and shared purpose reduce conflict and transaction costs, making collaboration easier both within and between organizations. The reduction of chronic stress and overwork—products of cultural conditions as much as individual choices—preserves the cognitive and creative capacity on which knowledge work depends. And organizations that attract and retain talented people by offering genuinely supportive cultures gain a compounding advantage over time.

More broadly, a flourishing society creates the human and cultural foundations on which sustainable economic growth depends. Economies built on the depletion of human well-being—on chronic overwork, on the erosion of trust, on the subordination of health and connection to short-term output—are consuming their own productive base. A culture that genuinely supports flourishing is, among other things, a strategy for long-term economic resilience.

7. The Effectiveness of Democratic Governance

Political thinkers have long recognized that the effectiveness of government depends heavily on the cultural environment in which it operates. Alexis de Tocqueville observed in the nineteenth century that the widespread habit of voluntary association strengthened American democracy: citizens who regularly worked together to address community challenges reduced reliance on centralized authority and strengthened civic responsibility. Robert D. Putnam's research demonstrated more recently that societies with high levels of social capital—trust, cooperation, and civic participation—tend to have more effective institutions and healthier democracies. The civic culture research of Gabriel Almond and Sidney Verba showed that stable democracies depend on citizens who trust institutions, participate constructively in civic life, and accept shared responsibility for the public good.

These insights converge on a principle with significant practical implications: strong cultures help societies govern themselves more effectively. When communities cultivate trust, cooperation, and shared values, government can focus less on managing social breakdown and more on stewarding long-term well-being. Conversely, when social trust erodes and cultural fragmentation deepens, the demands on government multiply even as the political conditions for effective governance deteriorate. The relationship between cultural health and governmental effectiveness is not incidental; it is structural.

A flourishing society builds on these insights by intentionally cultivating the cultural values—productive work, health, joy, kindness, learning, and connection—that strengthen the social foundations on which effective democratic governance depends. Cultural investment is, in this sense, also a civic investment.

Part II: Why This is Urgent

The problems described above are not new. Loneliness, crime, poor health, injustice, and weak civic institutions have been features of every society in every era. What has changed, and what makes the cultivation of flourishing cultures a matter of urgency now, is a convergence of conditions that simultaneously increase the scale of these problems, reduce the effectiveness of conventional responses, and create an unusual window of opportunity for cultural approaches.

The Scale of the Problems Has Reached Critical Thresholds

In many societies, the problems that flourishing cultures address have reached levels that stress conventional institutions to and beyond their capacity. Mental health systems in most developed countries are overwhelmed; demand for services consistently outpaces supply, and the gap is growing. Loneliness has been declared a public health epidemic in multiple countries—the economic costs of disengagement, chronic stress, and preventable illness run into trillions of dollars annually. Social trust—the foundation of both effective markets and effective government—has declined in most democracies over the past generation.

These are not problems that can be solved by expanding existing clinical, criminal justice, or social service systems. The systems themselves are products of the cultural conditions that produced the problems; they can ameliorate symptoms at the margin, but they cannot address root causes. The urgency lies in recognizing that we have reached a scale of social dysfunction that demands upstream, generative responses—and that cultural cultivation is among the most powerful available.

The Costs of Inaction are Compounding

Social problems of the kind described in this chapter are not static. They compound. Loneliness erodes health, which strains healthcare systems, which reduces the resources available for prevention, which deepens the conditions that produce loneliness. Crime and violence erode trust, which weakens the social cohesion that prevents crime, which produces more crime and violence. Mental illness, untreated, becomes chronic, which reduces economic participation, which increases financial stress, which worsens mental illness. These feedback loops mean that the cost of delay is not linear: problems left unaddressed do not simply persist at their current level; they grow and interconnect in ways that make them progressively harder and more expensive to address.

The cultural conditions that sustain flourishing operate by a similar logic but in the opposite direction. Trust generates cooperation, which produces shared resources and social capital, which makes further trust more rational. Communities that invest in the conditions for belonging find that belonging generates the civic participation and mutual accountability that make further investment more effective. The positive compounding effects of cultural health are as real as the negative compounding effects of cultural dysfunction—and they are equally available to those who choose to pursue them.

Conventional Approaches Have Reached Their Limits

The past several decades have seen significant investment in evidence-based programs to address the problems described in this chapter: cognitive-behavioral therapies, recidivism-reduction programs, anti-discrimination training, workplace wellness initiatives, and civic education curricula. These investments have produced genuine benefits at the individual and program level. What they have not done, for the most part, is change the cultural conditions that continue to produce the problems they address. They treat symptoms in individuals without changing the generative environment that produces those symptoms across populations.

This is not a criticism of the programs themselves; many are excellent. It is an observation about what they are designed to do. A well-designed cognitive-behavioral therapy helps an individual develop more effective responses to anxiety. It does not change the cultural norms that produce anxiety in that individual and in the thousands of others who share their environment. The urgency of cultural approaches lies precisely here: they operate at the level where individual-level interventions cannot reach, and they change the conditions under which such interventions must operate.

We Now Know Enough to Act

One of the most important developments of the past generation in the social sciences is the accumulation of high-quality evidence about which cultural conditions produce human flourishing and which undermine it. The research of Holt-Lunstad on social connection and health, Sampson on collective efficacy and public safety, Putnam on social capital and democratic effectiveness, Seligman on the conditions for psychological well-being, Ornish on the role of relationship in physical health, Allport on the conditions for prejudice reduction—this body of evidence, taken together, provides a substantially clearer picture of what a flourishing culture requires than any previous generation has had access to.

This knowledge carries with it a responsibility. When we know what produces human flourishing, and when the costs of failing to cultivate it are as clear and as large as they are, the failure to act becomes harder to justify on grounds of uncertainty. We are not waiting for more evidence. We are waiting for the will to act on the evidence we have.

The Window for Cultural Change is Open

Cultural change is difficult but not impossible, and there are periods when cultural conditions are more amenable to change than at other times. Significant social disruptions—technological change, demographic shifts, widespread experience of collective challenge—can loosen the grip of existing cultural patterns and create openings for the deliberate cultivation of new ones. Many societies are currently in such a period. The disruptions of recent decades—in technology, in economic structure, in demographic composition, in the experience of collective challenge—have unsettled existing cultural patterns in ways that create genuine possibilities for intentional cultural cultivation.

This window will not remain open indefinitely. Cultural patterns, once established or re-established, tend to become self-reinforcing. The choice facing societies now is not whether cultural change will occur—it is already occurring—but whether it will occur intentionally, in the direction of flourishing, or by default, in whatever direction the strongest short-term pressures happen to push.

Part III: What Flourishing Cultures Require

The preceding chapters have explained what it takes to cultivate a flourishing culture. This section offers a brief synthesis, organized around the conditions that all the evidence points toward as most essential.

Flourishing cultures require shared values that are operative, not merely declared. The values of productive work, health, joy, kindness, learning, and connection must be embedded in the incentive structures, recognition systems, leadership behaviors, and everyday norms that govern daily experience—not just in mission statements. The gap between stated and operative values, is often where the most important diagnostic information lives.

They require structural conditions that make flourishing possible, not just cultural exhortation. People cannot maintain health in environments that systematically destroy it. They cannot sustain a connection in structures that relentlessly isolate them. They cannot learn in cultures that punish the admission of error. Cultivating flourishing requires examining and changing the structural conditions—the policies, incentive systems, physical environments, and resource allocations—that either enable or foreclose the values being promoted.

They require leadership that models what it promotes. The signal value of leadership behavior is disproportionate: leaders who model flourishing values create permission for others to do the same, while leaders whose behavior contradicts stated values erode cultural trust in ways that take years to repair. The cultivation of flourishing cultures begins with cultivating leaders who genuinely embody them.

They require participatory processes that treat cultural change as something done with people, not to them. Culture change efforts that engage people as co-creators produce more durable results than those that implement change from above. The analysis, objective setting, and cultivation of flourishing work best when the people whose flourishing is at stake are involved in shaping them.

And they require sustained attention over time. Culture does not change in a quarter or a year. Evidence from effective cultural change consistently identifies duration, consistency, and willingness to revisit and adapt as among the most important predictors of lasting transformation. The cultivation of flourishing is not a project with a completion date; it is a practice with a direction.

Conclusion: The Case for Cultural Investment

This book argues that a flourishing society is not a utopia—it is not a society without conflict, suffering, or difficulty. It is a society that has deliberately cultivated the cultural conditions in which human beings are more likely to thrive: to work with purpose, to maintain health, to experience joy, to treat one another with kindness, to keep learning, and to build genuine connections with the people around them.

The evidence assembled in the chapters summarized here suggests that these cultural conditions have consequences that extend far beyond individual well-being. They shape the mental and physical health of populations. They determine whether communities are safe or violent, connected or isolated, just or unjust. They govern the effectiveness of economic organizations and democratic institutions. They are, in the most literal sense, the foundation on which everything else is built.

The case for treating cultural investment with the same seriousness that societies direct toward economic policy, public infrastructure, or national security is therefore not idealistic—it is practical. Economies that deplete their human foundations will eventually exhaust them. Democracies that allow their cultural foundations—trust, civic participation, shared purpose—to erode will eventually find that the institutions built on those foundations no longer function. The cultivation of flourishing is not a luxury that societies pursue when more urgent problems have been solved. It is among the most urgent problems there is.

The good news, and the reason this book has been written, is that the cultivation of flourishing is not beyond our reach. We know more about what it requires than any previous generation. We have tools for analysis, frameworks for change, and examples of communities and organizations that have achieved it. What remains is the commitment to treat cultural cultivation as the serious, sustained, evidence-based practice it requires. The final chapter asks what it looks like to honor that commitment—not at the level of society but in the specific cultural spaces each of us already inhabits.

Chapter 21

Cultivating a Flourishing Society: A Shared Invitation

We began with a simple but profound premise: many of the struggles people experience today are not merely personal shortcomings or isolated failures. They are often reflections of cultural environments that are misaligned with fundamental human needs. If cultures shape behavior and can be shaped, then flourishing is not accidental—it is intentional.

This book has argued that a flourishing society is possible. Not perfect. Not free of hardship. But organized around shared values that support productive work, health, joy, kindness, learning, and connection. When these values are embedded in norms, leadership practices, peer relationships, social climate, and reinforcing touchpoints, they become lived realities rather than abstract ideals.

This closing chapter steps back from the details of analysis, institutional design, and change methodology to ask what it all adds up to—what kind of society becomes possible when communities persistently and together choose to cultivate the conditions for human flourishing.

I. What We Have Learned About Culture

We explored culture not as decoration but as infrastructure.

Cultures and subcultures function like interconnected webs. Leadership signals shape norms. Norms influence peer expectations. Peer expectations affect social climate. Social climate determines whether individuals feel a sense of belonging, a shared direction, and realistic hope. Touchpoints—such as rewards, modeling, stories, policies, and everyday routines—reinforce what is truly valued.

When these strands align around survival, competition, fear, or fragmentation, even well-intentioned individuals struggle. When they align around dignity, contribution, health, and connection, people are quietly supported in becoming their best selves.

The deepest insight this framework offers is not about any single element but about their interdependence. A culture cannot be improved by adjusting one lever while leaving the others unchanged—shared values without reinforcing touchpoints remain aspirational; strong norms without leadership modeling erode under pressure; uplifting social climate without structural support is fragile. Lasting change requires attending to the whole system—values, norms, peer relationships, leadership behavior, structural touchpoints, and social climate—aligned around the same direction at the same time. That alignment is not a starting condition. It is the achievement.

II. The Role of Institutions

No society flourishes without healthy institutions. Families, schools, workplaces, civic organizations, healthcare systems, financial structures, governments, and technologies all transmit values and reinforce behaviors.

Each institution faces the same choice—to reinforce fragmentation or belonging, short-term gain or long-term well-being, isolation or connection, burnout or sustainable contribution—and makes that choice whether or not it does so consciously.

The question is not whether institutions shape culture—they always do. The question is whether they do so intentionally.

A flourishing society requires institutions that embody its values internally while advancing them externally. Governments that steward rather than dominate. Healthcare systems that promote prevention and dignity. Workplaces that align productivity with well-being. Technologies that amplify connection rather than division.

Institutional culture is the bridge between aspiration and lived experience.

III. How Change Happens

Change does not occur through inspiration alone. It requires structure.

Drawing from social innovation theory, diffusion principles, action research traditions, and normative systems thinking, we outlined a four-phase approach to intentional culture change:

1. **Analysis, objective setting, and leadership development:** Understanding the existing culture honestly, clarifying shared goals, and developing the credible leadership that makes change possible.
2. **Involvement:** Inviting the people whose flourishing is at stake to participate, listening to what they know, and building the shared ownership that makes change durable rather than imposed.

3. **Integration of cultural supports:** Aligning norms, touchpoints, peer practices, and leadership behaviors so that flourishing values are reinforced by the everyday environment rather than contradicted by it.
4. **Evaluation, celebration, and renewal:** Assessing what has changed, reinforcing what is working, and returning to the process with accumulated understanding rather than starting over.

Flourishing cultures are not declared; they are cultivated. What makes this process genuinely hopeful is that each phase prepares the ground for the next: honest analysis builds the shared understanding that makes ambitious goals credible; genuine involvement builds the ownership that sustains integration; careful integration creates the evidence that makes evaluation meaningful; and evaluation, done well, renews both the culture and the commitment to keep cultivating it.

IV. Why This Matters Now

The preceding chapter documented the scale of the social problems that cultural neglect produces and the compounding cost of delay. That argument is the case for urgency. This chapter is concerned with something different: not the argument for acting but the invitation to begin—and the recognition that beginning does not require waiting for society to move first. The question before us is whether we will allow culture to drift or intentionally shape it.

Flourishing is not naïve optimism. It is disciplined alignment. It is the recognition that human well-being depends not only on personal resilience but on supportive environments. It acknowledges that systems can either amplify stress or reduce it, either isolate individuals or connect them, either reward extraction or contribution.

V. The Power of Subcultures

Large-scale transformation rarely begins at the national level. It begins in subcultures.

A family that decides to make kindness and learning genuine daily priorities is cultivating a subculture. A team that actively normalizes peer support and honest feedback is cultivating a subculture. A department that adjusts how it recognizes contribution, or a civic group that models inclusive leadership, is doing the same. None of these efforts requires permission from above or resources from outside. They require only clarity about what matters, honesty about the gap between aspiration and current reality, and the willingness to close that gap deliberately.

Subcultures are laboratories of possibility. When aligned with flourishing values, they become demonstration sites that show change is achievable.

Over time, aligned subcultures accumulate. Norms shift. Expectations change. A tipping point emerges where flourishing becomes the default rather than the exception.

VI. A Shared Responsibility

No single leader, expert, or institution can create a flourishing society alone. The work is distributed.

Beginning does not require a mandate or a budget line. It begins with an honest question in the cultural space you already occupy: what do the people here actually experience, and what would it take to make that experience more consistently aligned with flourishing? That question, asked seriously and followed up with action, is the beginning of cultural cultivation.

We need not change everything. We can begin where we stand.

What this book has tried to provide are the tools for that reflection—ways of seeing culture clearly enough to design it intentionally, and ways of designing it intentionally enough that the values people hold can become the values the culture actually lives.

The invitation of this book is cooperative and systematic action—guided by shared values, informed by analysis, strengthened through partnership, and sustained through reinforcement.

VII. A Final Invitation

Flourishing is both deeply personal and profoundly collective. It honors individuality while recognizing interdependence. It seeks productivity without sacrificing health, joy without abandoning responsibility, and connection without suppressing diversity. Flourishing is not a slogan. It is a design challenge—one that every household, organization, community, and society faces, whether or not it chooses to meet it consciously.

The future will not be shaped solely by policies or technologies. It will be shaped by the cultural environments we build and sustain.

We can drift toward fragmentation.

Or we can design for flourishing.

The work is complex—but it is achievable. It is incremental—but cumulative. It is demanding—but hopeful.

A flourishing society is not a distant dream. It is a series of intentional choices, made together, across the cultures we inhabit every day.

The question is not whether culture shapes us.

The question is how we will shape it in return.

References

Because the book synthesizes ideas from several decades of social science rather than presenting original empirical research, many of its references are to seminal works in their fields.

Preface

Allen, R. F., & Kraft, C. (1980). *Beat the system: A way to create more human environments*. McGraw-Hill.

Chapter 1: Beyond Good Intentions: Cultivating a Society Where People Thrive

Allen, R. F., & Kraft, C. (1987). *The organizational unconscious: How to win the struggle for your company's culture*. Human Resources Institute.

Almond, G. A., & Verba, S. (1963). *The civic culture: Political attitudes and democracy in five nations*. Princeton University Press.

Bellah, R. N., Madsen, R., Sullivan, W. M., Swidler, A., & Tipton, S. M. (1991). *The good society*. Alfred A. Knopf.

Fromm, E. (1955). *The sane society*. Rinehart & Company.

Lewin, K. (1947). Frontiers in group dynamics: Concept, method and reality in social science; social equilibria and social change. *Human Relations, 1*(1), 5–41.

Lewin, K. (1951). *Field theory in social science: Selected theoretical papers*. Harper & Row.

Putnam, R. D. (2000). *Bowling alone: The collapse and revival of American community*. Simon & Schuster.

Chapter 3: The Role of Cultural Norms in a Flourishing Society

Edmondson, A. C. (1999). Psychological safety and learning behavior in work teams. *Administrative Science Quarterly*, 44(2), 350–383.

Edmondson, A. C. (2018). The fearless organization: *Creating psychological safety in the workplace for learning, innovation, and growth*. Wiley.

Chapter 4: The Role of Cultural Touchpoints in a Flourishing Society

Allen, R. F., & Kraft, C. (1987). *The organizational unconscious: How to win the struggle for your company's culture*. Human Resources Institute.

Chapter 7: The Role of Social Climate in a Flourishing Society

Allen, J. (2025). *Cultivating connections: Building supportive cultural environments in an age marked by loneliness, alienation, and distrust:* Human Resources Institute.

Chapter 8: The Role of Technology and Innovation in a Flourishing Society

Buolamwini, J., & Gebru, T. (2018). *Gender shades: Intersectional accuracy disparities in commercial gender classification*. Proceedings of Machine Learning Research, 81, 1–15.

Haugen, F. (2021). Facebook whistleblower Frances Haugen: The 60 Minutes interview [Television broadcast]. CBS News.

Chapter 12: The Role of Workplaces in a Flourishing Society

Coyle, D. (2018). *The culture code: The secrets of highly successful groups*. Bantam Books.

Chapter 16: Examples of Flourishing Cultures in Action

Buettner, D. (2012). *The blue zones: 9 lessons for living longer from the people who've lived the longest* (2nd ed.). National Geographic Society.

Edmondson, A. C. (1999). Psychological safety and learning behavior in work teams. *Administrative Science Quarterly, 44*(2), 350–383. [Google Project Aristotle context]

Google. (2016). *Project Aristotle: Understanding team effectiveness*. Google re: Work. https://rework.withgoogle.com/print/guides/5721312655835136/

Liker, J. K. (2004). *The Toyota way: 14 management principles from the world's greatest manufacturer*. McGraw-Hill.

Mandela, N. (1994). *Long walk to freedom: The autobiography of Nelson Mandela*. Little, Brown.

Whyte, W. F., & Whyte, K. K. (1988). *Making Mondragon: The growth and dynamics of the worker cooperative complex*. ILR Press.

Chapter 17: Deciding Where to Begin

Rogers, E. M. (2003). *Diffusion of innovations* (5th ed.). Free Press.

Chapter 18: Analyzing Flourishing in the Current Culture

Allen, R. F., & Kraft, C. (1987). *The organizational unconscious: How to win the struggle for your company's culture*. Human Resources Institute.

Lewin, K. (1947). Frontiers in group dynamics: Concept, method and reality in social science; social equilibria and social change. *Human Relations, 1*(1), 5–41.

Chapter 19: Embracing Systemic and Systematic Change

Allen, R. F., & Kraft, C. (1987). *The organizational unconscious: How to win the struggle for your company's culture*. Human Resources Institute.

Lewin, K. (1951). *Field theory in social science: Selected theoretical papers*. Harper & Row.

Rogers, E. M. (2003). *Diffusion of innovations* (5th ed.). Free Press.

Chapter 20: Why Flourishing Cultures Matter: A Summary of Social Science Evidence

Allport, G. W. (1954). *The nature of prejudice*. Addison-Wesley.

Almond, G. A., & Verba, S. (1963). *The civic culture: Political attitudes and democracy in five nations*. Princeton University Press.

Coyle, D. (2018). *The culture code: The secrets of highly successful groups*. Bantam Books.

de Tocqueville, A. (2000). *Democracy in America* (H. C. Mansfield & D. Winthrop, Trans.). University of Chicago Press. (Original work published 1835–1840)

Fromm, E. (1955). *The sane society*. Rinehart & Company.

Holt-Lunstad, J., Smith, T. B., & Layton, J. B. (2010). Social relationships and mortality risk: A meta-analytic review. *PLOS Medicine*, 7(7), e1000316. https://doi.org/10.1371/journal.pmed.1000316

Ornish, D., & Ornish, A. (2019). *Undo it! How simple lifestyle changes can reverse most chronic diseases*. Ballantine Books.

Putnam, R. D. (2000). *Bowling alone: The collapse and revival of American community*. Simon & Schuster.

Sampson, R. J., Raudenbush, S. W., & Earls, F. (1997). Neighborhoods and violent crime: A multilevel study of collective efficacy. *Science, 277*(5328), 918–924.

Seligman, M. E. P. (2011). *Flourish: A visionary new understanding of happiness and well-being*. Free Press.

Key Intellectual Influences

The ideas in *Cultivating a Flourishing Society* build on a long tradition of scholarship exploring how culture, institutions, and social relationships shape human well-being. Several thinkers have been especially influential in shaping the framework presented here.

Émile Durkheim – Social Integration and Anomie

Durkheim's foundational sociological work demonstrated that societies require shared norms and social integration to function well. When those bonds weaken, individuals experience anomie—a state of normlessness associated with anxiety, alienation, and social instability. A flourishing society maintains strong yet humane normative structures that support a sense of belonging and purpose.

Erich Fromm – Culture and Mental Health

In *The Sane Society*, Erich Fromm argued that widespread psychological distress often reflects unhealthy social arrangements rather than individual pathology. When societies prioritize status, competition, and consumption over connection, meaning, and dignity, alienation becomes predictable. This book extends that insight by asking how societies can deliberately cultivate cultural conditions that support flourishing.

Gabriel Almond and Sidney Verba – Civic Culture

In *The Civic Culture*, Almond and Verba showed that democratic stability depends not only on formal institutions but also on supportive cultural norms—trust, participation, moderation, and belief in collective efficacy. Their work demonstrates that political and social systems function best when culture supports responsible citizenship.

Kurt Lewin – Behavior and Social Environment

Social psychologist Kurt Lewin's field theory emphasized that behavior is a function of both individuals and their environments. His development of action research demonstrated how communities and organizations can systematically diagnose problems, test solutions, and learn from experience. Lewin's work provides a methodological foundation for intentional cultural change.

Robert F. Allen – Normative Systems and Cultural Architecture

Robert F. Allen's work on normative systems emphasized that culture is sustained by a network of expectations, reinforcements, and emotional signals that quietly guide behavior. His framework highlighted how leaders can align values, norms, and institutional practices so that desired behaviors become natural rather than forced.

Robert Putnam – Social Capital and Community Life

Robert Putnam's research on social capital, most famously in *Bowling Alone*, documented the consequences of declining civic participation and weakening community networks. His work highlights the importance of trust, association, and shared civic engagement in sustaining both democratic life and individual well-being.

Urie Bronfenbrenner – Ecological Systems of Human Development

Bronfenbrenner's ecological model showed how individual development is shaped by nested systems of influence—families, schools, communities, institutions, and broader culture. His framework reinforces the central premise of this book: flourishing emerges not only from personal effort but from supportive environments across multiple levels of society.

These traditions collectively lead to a shared conclusion: Human flourishing is not just an individual success; it is a cultural achievement. Societies that intentionally foster supportive norms, relationships, and institutions create conditions for people to thrive.

Appendix: The Case for Flourishing Values

Cultivating a Flourishing Society embraces six primary cultural values. The following pages examine why each of these values is essential to flourishing cultures. The culture change goal is to embed these values in the norms and support systems of our institutions and social relationships.

Joy

Joy is the shared commitment of a culture to creating and protecting the conditions in which people can experience deep, authentic delight in being alive—through meaningful relationships, beauty, play, celebration, and the felt sense that life is worth living. As a cultural value, joy is not the pursuit of pleasure or the avoidance of pain but the cultivation of a collective atmosphere in which wonder, gratitude, laughter, and aliveness are recognized as serious human goods worthy of communal investment and protection.

Joy is a foundational value for a flourishing society for several interconnected reasons:

It fuels prosocial behavior. Joyful people are more generous, cooperative, and empathetic. Positive emotions broaden our thinking and make us more likely to invest in others—building the social trust that holds communities together.

It sustains motivation and creativity. Joy isn't just pleasant; it's generative. People who find meaning and delight in their work and relationships produce more, innovate more, and persist through difficulty better. A society that cultivates joy keeps moving forward.

It's a signal of genuine flourishing. Metrics like GDP or productivity can mask deep social dysfunction. Joy—especially shared, communal joy—is harder to fake. When people genuinely experience it, it's evidence that basic needs, dignity, belonging, and purpose are being met.

It counteracts the corrosive effects of fear and resentment. Societies dominated by anxiety, grievance, or despair tend toward tribalism and conflict. Joy creates psychological space for tolerance, forgiveness, and openness to others—the conditions democracy and civil life depend on.

It's contagious in the best way. Research on emotional contagion shows that positive emotions spread through social networks. A culture that normalizes and celebrates joy tends to reproduce it—creating virtuous cycles of well-being rather than vicious ones of misery.

It connects us to meaning. At a deeper philosophical level, thinkers from Aristotle to contemporary positive psychologists argue that joy—especially the kind rooted in purpose, connection, and virtue—is not merely a byproduct of a good life but partly constitutive of it. A society that treats joy as frivolous tends to mistake busyness for progress and suffering for seriousness.

The key distinction worth making is between **shallow pleasure** (consumption, distraction) and **deep joy**—the kind that comes from love, contribution, beauty, and belonging. It's the latter that genuinely nourishes societies, and cultivating it requires real investment: in community, in fairness, and in the conditions in which people can truly thrive.

Learning

Learning is the shared commitment of a culture to remaining perpetually curious, humble, and open—cultivating in its people the desire and capacity to grow in understanding, skill, wisdom, and self-knowledge throughout their lives. As a cultural value, learning is not the accumulation of credentials or the mastery of prescribed content, but the cultivation of a collective disposition in which questioning, discovery, honest inquiry, and the willingness to be wrong are recognized as marks of strength, maturity, and genuine intelligence worthy of deep communal respect and investment.

Learning is one of the most vital values a flourishing society can cultivate, and here's why:

It's the engine of adaptation. The world changes constantly—technologically, ecologically, politically. Societies that prioritize learning can respond, evolve, and solve novel problems. Those that don't become brittle. The capacity to learn collectively is essentially a society's immune system against obsolescence and crisis.

It builds human dignity and agency. When people can learn—genuinely understand their world, develop skills, and engage with ideas—they become active participants in their own lives rather than passive subjects of forces they can't comprehend. Learning is inseparable from self-determination.

It sustains democracy. Democratic self-governance requires an informed, critically thinking citizenry. Without a culture of learning, democracies are vulnerable to manipulation, demagoguery, and the collapse of shared reality. Voters, jurors, and neighbors all need the capacity to reason carefully about complex issues.

It generates empathy and reduces prejudice. Encountering new ideas, histories, and perspectives—genuinely engaging with them—tends to soften rigid thinking and expand moral imagination. Learning is one of the most reliable paths to understanding people unlike ourselves, which is foundational to a pluralistic society.

It compounds over generations. Unlike many resources, knowledge grows when shared. A society that learns passes on accumulated wisdom, science, art, and hard-won lessons. Each generation inherits a richer starting point—provided that learning is valued enough to be transmitted faithfully and critically.

It cultivates humility. Deep learning consistently reveals how much we don't know. That humility—the recognition of complexity and uncertainty—is actually a social good. It makes people more open to evidence, more willing to revise views, and less susceptible to the dangerous certainty that drives fanaticism.

It connects joy to purpose. There's something intrinsically satisfying about understanding something you didn't before—the "aha" moment is one of the most universal human pleasures. A society that fosters learning aligns individual fulfillment with collective benefit, which is a rare and powerful thing.

It fights stagnation at every level. Whether in science, governance, the arts, or everyday relationships, growth requires the willingness to be wrong, to revise, and to incorporate new understanding. Without learning as a core value, institutions calcify and cultures stagnate.

The deeper point is that learning isn't just about acquiring information—it's about developing the **character to stay curious, humble, and open** throughout life. A society full of people like that can navigate almost anything.

Connection

Connection is the shared commitment of a culture to fostering the conditions in which people experience genuine belonging—cultivating in its people the capacity and opportunity to know and be known by others in relationships of authentic mutual care, recognition, and solidarity across difference. As a cultural value, connection is not the accumulation of contacts or the performance of sociability, but the cultivation of a collective atmosphere in which people are truly seen, genuinely valued, and meaningfully bound to one another and to something larger than themselves—recognized as a fundamental human need worthy of the deepest communal investment and protection.

Connection may be the most foundational value of all for a flourishing society—because without it, the other values struggle to take root. There are multiple reasons why:

It's the basis of all social trust. Trust—the willingness to rely on and be vulnerable to others—doesn't emerge from institutions or laws alone. It grows from genuine human connection. And without trust, cooperation breaks down, markets fail, governance corrupts, and communities fragment. Connection is the soil in which trust grows.

It directly shapes health and well-being. The evidence here is striking. Loneliness and social isolation are as damaging to physical health as smoking or obesity. Conversely, people with strong social bonds live longer, recover from illness faster, and report higher life satisfaction. A society of disconnected individuals is a sick society in the most literal sense.

It transforms strangers into neighbors. Abstract compassion for "humanity" is hard to sustain. But connection—knowing someone's name, story, and struggle—makes moral concern concrete and durable. Neighbors look out for each other. Strangers often don't. Connection is what closes the gap between the two.

It makes solidarity possible. When people feel genuinely connected to one another, sacrifice for the common good becomes imaginable. They pay taxes that benefit others, volunteer, and show up in crisis. Disconnected societies struggle to mobilize collective action precisely because the "we" that makes sacrifice meaningful has dissolved.

It counters the politics of resentment. Much of what drives social polarization and extremism is the pain of feeling unseen, unvalued, and alone. Connection—real, mutual recognition between people—is one of the most powerful antidotes to the grievance and alienation that demagogues exploit. It's hard to dehumanize someone you're genuinely connected to.

It transmits culture and wisdom. Knowledge, values, and meaning don't travel through texts alone—they travel through relationships. Mentorship, storytelling, shared ritual, and intergenerational bonds are all forms of connection that carry a society's deepest wisdom forward. Sever those connections, and the transmission breaks down.

It amplifies joy and softens suffering. Pleasure shared is pleasure deepened. Pain carried alone is pain magnified. Connection doesn't eliminate hardship, but it changes its texture entirely. Grief shared in community, celebration shared with friends—these experiences remind us that we are not alone in the human condition, which is itself profoundly sustaining.

It gives individuals a sense of meaning. Psychologists consistently find that close relationships are the single strongest predictor of a meaningful life—more than achievement, wealth, or status. A society that systematically undermines connection—through overwork, digital isolation, urban atomization—is quietly bankrupting its people of meaning, even as material conditions improve.

It makes difference livable. Pluralistic societies must find ways to hold genuine disagreement and diversity together without fracturing. Connection—not agreement but real relationship—is what makes that possible. You can disagree deeply with someone you're connected to. It's much harder to live peacefully beside someone who is simply a stranger or an abstraction.

The thread running through all of this is that **human beings are fundamentally relational creatures.** We don't just happen to benefit from connection—we are, in a deep sense, constituted by it. Our identities, our values, our capacity for joy and resilience all emerge through relationships. A society that honors that truth and actively cultivates connection isn't just being sentimental—it's being wise about what human life actually requires to flourish.

Kindness

Kindness is the shared commitment of a culture to seeing and responding to the full humanity of every person—cultivating in its people the disposition to extend genuine care, generosity, and compassionate attention to others, including strangers and those who are difficult to love, not as a social nicety or performance of virtue but as a profound moral orientation that recognizes the dignity, vulnerability, and worth of every human being as inherently deserving of tenderness and goodwill. As a cultural value, kindness is not about weakness or sentimentality. It is about the cultivation of a collective character in which the suffering of others is taken seriously, the struggles of others are met with grace, and the presence of others is received as a gift worthy of genuine welcome and care.

Kindness is often underestimated as a social value—dismissed as soft or sentimental—but it may be one of the most practically powerful forces a society can cultivate. Here's why:

It's the everyday currency of civilization. Grand virtues like justice and courage matter enormously, but most of life is made up of small moments—how you speak to a colleague, whether you hold the door, how you treat someone having a bad day. Kindness is the value that governs those moments, and cumulatively, those moments *are* the texture of social life. A society rich in small kindnesses is a profoundly different place to inhabit than one that lacks them.

It creates psychological safety. When people know they will be treated with basic decency, they open up—they take risks, admit mistakes, ask for help, and engage honestly. Kindness lowers the social temperature in ways that make collaboration, creativity, and genuine communication possible. Harshness, by contrast, makes people defensive and small.

It interrupts cycles of harm. Much cruelty is perpetuated not by monsters but by ordinary people responding to their own pain, stress, or indifference. A single act of unexpected kindness can break that cycle—disarming hostility, softening hardened attitudes, and reminding someone of their own capacity for goodness. Kindness is quietly subversive in this way.

It scales trust without requiring institutions. Laws and institutions can enforce minimum standards of behavior, but they can't manufacture genuine care. Kindness does something institutions can't—it signals that another person sees you as fully human and worthy of consideration. That recognition builds the kind of deep social trust that no policy can manufacture from the top down.

It's morally contagious. Research consistently shows that witnessing kindness inspires kindness in others—even in observers who weren't directly involved. One generous act ripples outward in ways the original actor never sees. A society that models and celebrates kindness is effectively seeding itself with more of it.

It protects the vulnerable without requiring heroism. Justice systems and safety nets are essential, but they're blunt instruments. Kindness operates at the granular level where vulnerable people actually live—the lonely elderly neighbor, the struggling student, the grieving coworker. It fills the gaps that formal structures can never fully reach, and it does so through ordinary people making ordinary choices.

It sustains relationships through inevitable friction. No community—family, workplace, neighborhood, nation—avoids conflict. What determines whether those communities survive and deepen is whether people extend goodwill and charitable interpretation to one another when things get hard. Kindness is the lubricant that keeps the machinery of relationships from grinding itself apart.

It reflects and reinforces human dignity. At its core, kindness is an acknowledgment that the person in front of you matters—that their comfort, their pain, their humanity is worth attending to. A culture that practices kindness is one that continuously reaffirms the equal worth of persons, not just in law or rhetoric but in lived daily experience.

It's good for the giver, too. This is often overlooked. Acts of kindness reliably increase the well-being, sense of purpose, and even physical health of the person performing them. Kindness isn't a sacrifice of self-interest—it's one of the most reliable paths to a genuinely satisfying life. A society that cultivates it creates conditions for flourishing at the individual and collective levels.

It resists the logic of pure transaction. Modern life is deeply shaped by market thinking—everything is evaluated in terms of utility, exchange, and return on investment. Kindness operates by a different logic entirely. It gives without calculating. It treats people as ends in themselves rather than means. In doing so, it preserves a domain of human life that pure transactionalism would otherwise colonize and impoverish.

The deeper truth about kindness is that it is not weakness dressed up as virtue—it is a form of moral courage and attention. It requires noticing others, resisting the pull of indifference, and choosing to act on behalf of someone else's well-being even when you don't have to. A society that takes that seriously is one that has understood something essential about what it means to live well together.

Health

Health is the shared commitment of a culture to creating and sustaining the conditions in which every person can experience the full vitality of their physical, mental, emotional, and spiritual being—cultivating in its people the capacity to live with energy, clarity, resilience, and wholeness across the full arc of their lives. As a cultural value, health is not the pursuit of bodily perfection or the mere absence of illness but the cultivation of a collective environment in which the complete well-being of every person is recognized as a profound communal responsibility—one that demands serious investment in the social, relational, environmental, and institutional conditions that make genuine flourishing possible for all, not merely for those with the means to purchase it.

Health is not merely one value among many in a flourishing society—it is in many ways the precondition for all the others. Here's why:

It is the foundation on which everything else is built. Joy, learning, connection, kindness—all are profoundly harder to sustain when people are sick, in pain, or exhausted. Health isn't just a personal good; it's the platform on which human capacity rests. A society that neglects health is quietly undermining every other value it claims to hold.

It is a precondition for genuine freedom. We talk a great deal about liberty in political life, but freedom without health is largely theoretical. A person too ill to work, too pain-ridden to think clearly, or too anxious about medical costs to take risks is not truly free in any meaningful sense. Health is what makes freedom livable rather than merely formal.

It sustains productive and creative capacity. Healthy people learn better, work more effectively, parent more patiently, and contribute more fully to their communities. The economic argument for health investment is overwhelming—but more fundamentally, human potential cannot be realized in bodies and minds that are neglected or broken down. Health unlocks what people can become.

It builds resilience against collective shocks. Pandemics, environmental disasters, and social crises all hit societies with poor baseline health harder. A population physically and mentally healthy has reserves—biological, psychological, and social—to draw on when things go wrong. Neglecting health in ordinary times is borrowing against a debt that will come due in the worst moments.

It is inseparable from mental and emotional well-being. The artificial separation of physical and mental health is one of the great mistakes of modern medicine and policy. Chronic physical illness drives depression and anxiety. Mental suffering manifests in physical symptoms. A society serious about health understands it holistically—as the full flourishing of body, mind, and spirit—and invests accordingly in both.

It shapes the character of public life. Societies with high rates of chronic pain, addiction, untreated mental illness, and health insecurity tend toward despair, short-term thinking, and social fragmentation. People consumed by survival cannot easily invest in the long-term common good. Health, broadly distributed, creates the psychological conditions for civic engagement, generosity, and the kind of forward-looking thinking that sustains great societies.

It is a measure of how well a society cares for its most vulnerable. Children, older adults, people with disabilities, and the chronically ill depend on collective investment in health more than most. How a society treats these groups—whether it surrounds them with care or leaves them exposed—reveals its deepest values. Commitment to health is commitment to the principle that vulnerability does not diminish worth.

It connects generations. The health choices and investments a society makes today—in nutrition, environment, maternal care, childhood development—ripple forward across decades. Healthy children become healthy adults who raise healthy children. Neglect compounds just as powerfully in the other direction. Health is one of the most important gifts one generation can offer the next.

It requires and reinforces solidarity. No one earns their genetic inheritance, the family they're born into, or the environmental conditions of their childhood. Health is partly a matter of individual choice, but far more deeply, it is a matter of circumstance, which means a flourishing society takes collective responsibility for it. The willingness to fund, build, and sustain systems of shared health is one of the highest expressions of social solidarity.

It makes the other values sustainable over a lifetime. Joy fades under chronic illness. Learning is stunted by untreated mental illness. Connection wanes when pain and exhaustion dominate. Kindness is harder to practice when you are depleted. Health is not just one value alongside the others—it is what allows all the others to be practiced consistently, deeply, and across the full arc of a human life.

The profound insight at the heart of valuing health is this: **a society does not simply have healthy or unhealthy individuals—it produces health or illness through its structures, priorities, and choices.** The built environment, the food system, the workplace, the quality of air and water, the availability of care—all of these are social decisions. A society that takes flourishing seriously understands that health is not a private matter to be left to individual willpower but a shared project that reflects and shapes everything else about how people live together.

Important Work

Important work is the shared commitment of a culture to ensuring that every person has the opportunity to contribute their distinctive gifts, talents, and energies toward something genuinely needed by the world—cultivating in its people the sense of vocation, craftsmanship, and purposeful effort that comes from knowing that what they do matters, that it is done well, and that it serves something beyond their own private interest. As a cultural value, important work is not the glorification of busyness, productivity, or economic output but the cultivation of a collective environment in which every person's capacity to contribute meaningfully is recognized as a profound human need and social treasure—one that demands serious investment in the conditions that allow people to discover, develop, and dedicate themselves to work that is worthy of their full humanity and genuinely worthy of the world's need.

Important work is one of the most underappreciated foundations of a flourishing society—because it speaks not just to what gets done but to how people find meaning, dignity, and purpose in their lives. Here's why:

It gives people a reason to get up in the morning. This is not trivial. Psychologists consistently find that a sense of purpose—feeling that what you do matters—is one of the strongest predictors of psychological well-being, resilience, and longevity. Important work provides that anchor. A society that gives its people access to meaningful contribution has solved one of the deepest problems of human existence.

It channels human energy toward collective benefit. People are capable of extraordinary effort, creativity, and sacrifice—but only when they believe what they're doing matters. Important work harnesses that capacity and directs it toward the things a society actually needs: healing the sick, educating children, building infrastructure, creating beauty, advancing knowledge, caring for the vulnerable. The alignment of individual effort with genuine social need is one of the great achievements a society can aspire to.

It is a primary source of human dignity. There is something profound about the experience of doing something well that the world needs done. Craftsmanship, expertise, dedication—these are not just economically valuable, they are expressions of human worth. A society that honors important work honors the people doing it, and in doing so affirms that contribution and competence are worthy of recognition and respect.

It counteracts meaninglessness and despair. Many of the deepest social pathologies of modern life—addiction, nihilism, political extremism, chronic depression—are rooted at least partly in a sense of purposelessness. When people feel their work is trivial, their contribution invisible, or their effort disconnected from anything that truly matters, something in them quietly dies. Important work is one of the most powerful antidotes to that spiritual emptiness.

It creates a sense of shared mission. When people understand that their work contributes to something larger than themselves—a healthier community, a more just society, a better-educated generation—it binds them together in a common project. That sense of shared purpose is one of the things that makes a collection of individuals into a genuine society. It transforms "I" into "we" through meaningful effort.

It elevates the quality of what gets done. People who believe their work matters bring more of themselves to it—more care, more creativity, more persistence. A society that cultivates a culture of important work doesn't just benefit morally; it benefits practically. The doctor who sees medicine as a calling, the teacher who understands that a child's future is in their hands, the engineer who grasps the human stakes of what they're building—all of them do better work than those who are merely going through the motions.

It distributes agency and responsibility broadly. A flourishing society is not one in which a small elite makes all the important decisions and everyone else executes instructions. It is one where people at every level understand that their work has genuine stakes, that their judgment matters, and that they bear real responsibility for outcomes. Important work is what makes ordinary people into genuine participants in the shared project of civilization rather than passive instruments of someone else's vision.

It sustains institutions and expertise across generations. The knowledge, skill, and dedication required to do important work well—in medicine, in law, in teaching, in governance, in the trades—is accumulated slowly and lost quickly. A society that values important work invests in passing on that accumulated excellence. It creates apprenticeships, honors mastery, and builds the institutional memory that allows each generation to begin from a higher starting point rather than reinventing everything from scratch.

It makes sacrifice intelligible and sustainable. Important work often demands real cost—long hours, difficult conditions, emotional weight, deferred reward. People will bear those costs willingly, even gratefully, when they understand why the work matters. The nurse who works exhausting shifts, the soldier who accepts danger, the teacher who spends their own money on classroom supplies—none of them are being exploited if they genuinely understand and embrace the importance of what they do. Meaning transforms burden into vocation.

It connects the individual to something that outlasts them. One of the deepest human longings is to contribute something that endures—to matter beyond the span of a single life. Important work offers that. The bridge an engineer designs, the students a teacher shapes, the research a scientist advances, the justice a lawyer wins—these ripple forward in ways the individual may never fully see. A society rich in important work is one that gives its people a genuine stake in the future.

It requires and reveals character. Doing important work well—with integrity, care, and genuine commitment—is not just technically demanding. It is morally demanding. It requires honesty about failure, courage to speak difficult truths, humility to keep learning, and the discipline to show up consistently over a long time. In this sense, important work doesn't just benefit society; it forms the people doing it, cultivating exactly the virtues a flourishing society depends on.

It bridges personal fulfillment and social contribution. One of the great tensions in any society is between what individuals want for themselves and what the community needs from them. Important work, at its best, dissolves that tension. When a person's deepest talents and passions are aligned with genuine social need, self-interest and altruism point in the same direction. That alignment is rare and precious—and a flourishing society works actively to create the conditions where more people can find it.

The deepest truth about important work is this: **human beings are not merely consumers of experience—they are makers, contributors, and builders who need to give as much as they need to receive.** A society that understands this creates structures, cultures, and opportunities that allow its people not just to be served but to serve—not just to benefit from civilization but to actively build and sustain it. That is what transforms a society from a marketplace into a genuine community of shared purpose and mutual investment in one another's flourishing.

The Overlapping Values of a Flourishing Society

Looking across the six values—**joy, learning, connection, kindness, health, and important work**—my honest assessment is that none of them is truly redundant, because each does something the others cannot. But if pressed, the strongest case for overlap is between kindness and connection.

Here's why someone might argue that:

Connection is the broader relational value—the fact of being genuinely bound to others in community. Kindness could be seen as simply the *behavioral expression* of connection—what connection looks like in action, moment to moment. If you have a deep, genuine connection, doesn't kindness follow naturally? And if kindness is just connection made manifest, is it doing independent work as a value in itself?

But I think that argument ultimately fails, for a few reasons:

- Kindness can and should extend *beyond* those we are connected to—to strangers, to people we will never meet, even to those we actively dislike. Connection is relational and particular; kindness is more universal in its reach.
- You can have connection without kindness—tight-knit communities can be deeply cruel to outsiders, and even loving relationships can harbor unkindness. They are genuinely distinct.
- Kindness is also an *internal disposition*—a way of perceiving others charitably—not just a social bond. That makes it irreducibly its own value.

So the more honest answer is that the six values form a remarkably non-redundant, interlocking set—each one addressing a different dimension of what flourishing actually requires. They overlap and reinforce each other beautifully, but none can be collapsed into another without losing something essential.

www.ingramcontent.com/pod-product-compliance
Lightning Source LLC
LaVergne TN
LVHW030917080826
845145LV00013B/2931

* 9 7 8 0 9 4 1 7 0 3 1 7 8 *